THE
FINGERPRINTS
OF GOD

Inspirational memoirs from a mother's heart

WENDEE BROWN

G od's Fingerprints are everywhere. We just need to pause and listen for His sweet voice whispering to us, "That was Me."

DISCLAIMER

The names have been changed to protect people's identity.

DEDICATION

—⟨𝓃⟩—

I dedicate this book to the loves and cheering squad of my life. My husband and biggest fan Greg, my two sons Christopher, (and wife Shelly Girl) Joshua (and wife Judy), my three daughters Tami (and husband Matt), Jessica (and husband Aaron), and Faith, our youngest and my right hand gal throughout the tedious process of prepping and grooming this manuscript for the press. Faith, I could not have done this without your tremendous help. I am humbled by how much you all believe in me that I could actually complete this dream. To all of my family I say:

I love you all for gently placing your hands into my tender heart and passing over all the weak lumpy bumpy things that I possess and for drawing out into the light all the lovely belongings that only one's own children and husband seem to find. You are indeed the loves of my life. I love you ever so deeply.

ACKNOWLEDGMENTS

—◦◦◦—

I would first like to thank my family for granting me the permission of opening wide the private curtain of our family life.

I would like to thank my best friend and journey traveler, Sally, for continually defining for me the words: 'loyal friend.' I thank my sister, Dawn, for always making me laugh, helping me fulfill one of my bucket list dreams- going cross county skiing, and for showing to the world what the gift of giving truly looks like. I thank my dear friends Ron and Diane (my "pajamas and no make-up" friends), for so powerfully reflecting God's love, especially when we had nothing to give in return. I thank my cousin, Julie, (the oldest friend and cousin I have) we met when we were two and played together every day of our childhood! To Leah, my niece—I will always remember the night we prayed and you gave your heart to Jesus. I also want to thank my Pastors Jamey and Nicole, for so graciously joining me in this dream of mine. I thank Renee and Michelle, my publishing consultants, who took time to answer my numerous questions sometimes what seemed daily. Many thanks to all the staff at Xulon Press for helping me fulfill this life long dream. Above all, I thank my Lord Jesus. To God be all the Glory forever and ever!

FOREWORD
By Faith Angelina Brown

My lovely mother and I have walked quite a road together. I would say that no one truly knows me better than she does. It gets ridiculous when we can finish each other's sentences and know what the other is thinking in a particular moment. An example of this would be any particularly hot summer day. My mom will turn to me and say, "You know what I really feel like having right now?" My immediate response is, "A root beer float?" There I am, at Cub, buying some ice cream and root beer. Simple little spontaneous things like that create the most beautiful memories. Although my mom doesn't like to admit it, she can indeed be spontaneous. Not all of our wonderful memories together were planned out. I remember this one night when we were baking some sweets in the kitchen. I had the music really loud and was taking requests from her on what to play. She had suggested some Motown, which is her favorite music to dance to. As I began playing all the "Motown Classic Hits," my mom was dancing away. For a second I thought, "What in the world is she doing?" Then I realized that she was actually teaching me one of the most important lessons in this world, to live in the moment. Upon realizing what she was doing, I set my ego aside and began to dance with her. We danced in that kitchen for two whole hours, but it felt like we had been dancing for ten minutes. I will never forget that night. It was a moment in time when the whole world stopped and it was just the two of us.

Enjoying the beauty of this world and living in the moment are my mom's specialties. She continues to point out the best in the world and the best in people. Without even thinking about it, my mom can easily bring out your best quality. She'll always build you up and be that listening ear that you need. I am very much a black and white person; my mom has taught me how to live life in color. She's also taught me not to take life too seriously, which I tend to do a lot.

My mom is a wonderful woman. We are very blessed with her as the matriarch of our family. My mom has a lot of love and life to fill this world with. I am so thankful that she wrote this book. I hope you enjoy reading all of my mom's colorful and wise stories. May this book bless you with a little extra color in your life.

Faith Brown

—⟨ഗ⟩—

"Keep your eyes open for God; watch for His works; be alert for signs of His presence. Remember the world of wonders He has made, His miracles, and the verdicts He has rendered."

Psalm 105: 2 The Message Bible

Webster defines the word "Vignette" as: 'a small decorative design- a short descriptive literary sketch.'

I guess that pretty much sums up this book I have written.

It all began when my oldest daughter, Tami, was in a bookstore and the Lord told her to purchase a particular book for me, 'to jumpstart me to write my own book.' I enjoyed the book immensely. So I continued writing and journaling my little heart out.

What follows is approximately 22 years of writings from my walk in this world. The writings are really quite a hodge-podge in style- or in culinary terms, a Hobo Stew. I hope that some of this will catch your fancy and perhaps leave some footprints on your heart. So scoop up a few servings in your bowl, then sit back and digest its contents.

INTRODUCTION

How does one begin and end a book of this sort? My life is continuously changing, stretching and growing. I am forever amazed, intertwined and aware of the many pieces that make up one's own individual quilt- and like antenna that protrude from a butterfly, I feel deeply and think long. Thus my writings are various in content. Some are poetic; some simply express an emotion from my heart on a particular subject- still some express a common aspect of life some of you will be quite familiar with and be able to relate to immediately- As you read, you will begin to see how life is constantly trying to pull us into society's carnal views, but how stronger still is the pull of the Lord's, which says to us, "Come, take my hand, trust Me, for I am for you and love you most unconditionally." It is my prayer that you will come to know that all of life must be rooted in the knowing deep inside that the King of Kings and Lord of Lords is sovereign over our lives; and that He is in constant search for us to take His hand and travel with Him. He will make Footprints in our Hearts for Eternity.

So please sit for a spell and enjoy the heart of Dee.

Side note: One day, in the middle of all the numerous literary responsibilities I was being faced with, feeling like I was drowning in a 10-foot wave, I heard my Lord Jesus softly encourage me. "I like your book." It was then that I received renewed energy. To know that my Lord had endorsed my book gave me incentive to finish strong.

CONTENTS

———✺———

Contents

Contents

Contents

Contents

RACHEL'S COMMENTARY

'I just love Grandma, she's so like WOW'!

How refreshing to hear a description of how my 6-year-old granddaughter sees me. I have been thinking about it. For a moment or two, I put her little glasses on. I see a grandma very much like my own mother was to my children. It is strange, but almost like I am reading a script and playing a part that has previously been written, or walking along a path that has previously been trodden. So the "WOW" that little Rachel sees in me so vividly, has traveled three generations back. I suddenly feel, well, like I have been defined. I love it!

Here I am with my Sweet Rachie Bach – all grown up now! June 2015

Here's those famous 'Dandelions and Dixie Cups' I received from my little sweethearts.

Our daughter, Jessica, husband Aaron, and granddaughters Natalie, Meg Rose, Kalia and Paige

LIFE'S CONTRASTS

I am always astounded by the many contrasts of life: one couple is vacationing in Italy, seeing all the sights and living it up, while on the opposite side of town there is a family struggling for a thread of hope in a difficult diagnosis. Someone has just received a miracle, someone has just been admitted to ICU, someone just gave birth to a new baby girl, and still someone else is lonely and feels no hope to hold on to.

Is life fair? No, but our Lord Jesus promises us He has a plan—the BIG Picture. That is how life makes sense.

WHEN IS ENOUGH, ENOUGH?

―⟐⟐⟐―

I am learning, though I wanted to prove it to be false, that nothing is ever enough- bigger homes, fancier cars, and even the "changing of the guard" in friendships. As a natural organizer, when I am completely finished with every possible thing I could organize, sift through, clean, and throw away, I strive for just "one more thing" to organize. When I have purchased that perfect pair of shoes, blouse, skirt, or dress, it is only for a short time that I think I have plenty of clothes; then the search begins all over again. Even when my yard is at its best—with flowers, hanging baskets on my porch, and cedar chips surrounding the trees and shrubs—new ideas seem to crop up like seedlings in the garden. When is enough, enough? Well, there is only one situation that I can answer "Yes" to this age old question.

When Jesus takes over. My mother used to say, "Contentment is next to Godliness." When I point my eyes to Jesus, I realize that it is *all* His—every bit of it—gratitude for everything loaned to me takes on a new meaning. I see "stuff" as gifts from Him—totally unearned, yet graciously given. It is said: "Jesus is our portion." Amen! He fills that space that a new pair of shoes will never permanently fill. You know, come to think of it, the "I want more" syndrome does have one positive attribute: once you have Jesus, you want more and more and more of Him!

BEWARE OF THE SNIPER ATTACK
6/01/08

—⚬⚬⚬—

L ife holds pitfalls, dark and deep forests, slippery walkways, steep paths, jagged rocks, scary cliffs, and "snipers". Snipers are people and events that are directed, staged, and produced fully by the enemy of our soul and his cast and crew of vipers. Sometimes we are caught off guard, when our heart is exposed, relaxed and trusting. This morning I got hit. I am down, but I am being lifted up. I cannot go on, but yes I can. I want to give up, but I will pray. Life is full of battles and He who owns the cattle on a thousand hills and remembers the number of hairs of my head, will uphold me. I will see Him face to face some day soon and I will understand it all.

"Be sober, be vigilant, because your adversary, the devil, walks about like a roaring lion seeking whom he may devour. Resist him, steadfast in the faith, knowing that the same sufferings are experienced by your brotherhood in the world" (1 Peter 5:8–9 NKJV).

VERY SPECIAL STORY ABOUT SOME VERY SPECIAL CHILDREN

October 20th, 2006

—⁓—

I t is Friday evening and I am babysitting for my grandbabies. I am putting Rachel and Josiah to bed. They are all jammied and I have just finished singing a made-up song to them. Rachel announces she wants to sing a song to me. So I place her in her bed next to Josiah. She begins her sweet precious song in a soft gentle and melodious sort of way. Random words spill forth, like 'Grandma sews for me. She's a good sewer. So is Nanna. Grandma and Bompa are married. They first dated then got married.'

My eyes well with tears, so I interrupt after a bit and thank her. I tell her that her song made me cry. I ask her if that is okay? She next pulls my hair behind my ears so she can see my face-then I bury my head on her shoulder and weep. When I bring my head up, she looks at me and begins to cry as well- her eyes welling up like pools. Now we both are crying. Then I look at her and say, 'Rachel, you have great compassion.'

To think that at 4 years old she would so empathize with her grandma that she would cry WITH me. Wow! What a magic moment that was for me. I love my little Rachies so very much.

"Then Jesus called a little child to Him, set him in the midst of them, and said, "Assuredly, I say to you, unless you are converted and become as little children you will by no means enter the kingdom of heaven, Therefore whoever humbles himself as this little child is the greatest in the kingdom of heaven. Whoever receives one little child like this in My name receives Me.'" (Matt. 18:2–5 NKJV).

THE WAKE UP CALL
written on Good Friday, April 14, 1995

—⚬⚬⚬—

On March 26th 1995 Greg and I drove to Wisconsin (directly from church). The plan was to be with my sister, Dawn, before, during and after her surgery. On Tuesday, March 28th, she was scheduled to have a cluster of fibroids removed. She had faithfully taken a drug named Lupron (used to shrink the fibroids) so surgery could be performed. She'd also been given 2 units of blood in preparation. We made plans for picking her up at 5:45 AM the next morning- surgery day.

Early the next day, we were greeted by Dawn's cheery face saying, "I'm running a little late." She hurried along (put on some make-up) and we were off to Elm Brook Memorial Hospital. When we arrived, they immediately put her ID wrist- band on- then escorted us to a small hospital room complete with a bed, TV and bathroom. She proceeded to get dressed in the hospital gown. Then I read some verses out of the Bible to her. (the nurse thought I was her pastor) They started her IV and also put these tight leg stockings on her (to prevent blood clotting) and help circulation. Eventually, they wheeled Dawn away (but not before we prayed to Jesus to watch over her). She was put in a holding partition. My husband, Greg, and I left to get her flowers and breakfast. Then we went to the waiting room. They'd told Dawn the surgery would be about 2 hours. After 3 hours, the receptionist told me the surgical nurse was on the phone and wanted to talk to me. I took the phone and was told they had a 'mish/mesh' in there and that it would be at least another hour and a half. I began to get nervous and prayed to the Lord to take care of my Dawn. She had been in surgery 4 hours when 2 doctors walked over to us and escorted us into a small conference room. One was Dawn's doctor, the other, an oncologist. They got right to the point and said they'd found a gross tumor (sarcoma—a bad cancer). 'It could take her out of this world,' was what was told to us. I felt all the pain of what seemed the whole world resting on my heart in those short yet furious moments. I remember thinking, 'Let me see my sister. I have to see my sister. Has she been told? Does she know?' They did not stay long and we were left to this bleak reality of cancer. My sister has cancer. We prayed and then went to her hospital room to await her arrival. It wasn't very long before they wheeled her in. She'd been told about the tumor but not that it was cancer. The doctor said he'd be in that evening. I held her close and tried my hardest to be strong. That evening the news was given to Dawn. I held Greg's hand tightly and shook like a leaf as we sat in the corner and the Dr. gave her the grim news. She had so many questions, to which he could not answer until the pathology tests came back. He stayed 1 ½ hours trying his best to reassure Dawn and not jump to conclusions. He told us the next 3 days will be a long 3 days as we await the results. We all went through the motions of existing, trying our best to eat, sleep, to keep that stiff upper lip for Dawn- and to pray, pray, pray. I contacted my best friend and told her to pray. Prayers were bombarding heaven. Finally, Friday morning arrived. At 9:15 AM the doctor walked in and Dawn immediately begged, "Doctor, don't tell me I'm going to die—I don't want any bad news." But the doctor said he had some good news. I held Dawn's hand tightly as he first announced that it was cancer—endometrial stripe sarcoma. However, he said that no cancer cells were found in the lymph nodes, that it was a low grade cancer, and that they were amazed Lupron had shrunk it- meaning that she could use Lupron or radiation, but not chemo. We were praising the Lord. Dawn was relieved but still very worried she would die.

Later that day, she returned to her home and Greg and I brought all her beautiful flowers there. You should have seen all her flowers she'd received in the hospital. I fixed her some food and she ate. On Saturday, we spent the day with her.

Later that evening, Greg and I returned home to be with our family. I still felt in shock over everything that had transpired. Each morning I'd wake, knowing my sister had cancer. So Sunday came and went. Monday I returned to work, and so the week went. But on Thursday afternoon at approximately 12:20 the phone rang at work. The call was for me. I took the phone to hear Dawn's voice. "Hello my beautiful gorgeous wonderful fantastic sister- how are you?" I mumbled that I was okay. She then proceeded to tell me to sit down. I did. She then said that the doctor had just called her. He said, 'Dawn, I bet you could use some good news. All the lab tests just arrived back and you do NOT have cancer. It is known as a degenerative fibroid.' As Dawn's words gently fell on my heart, I began crying- and praising Jesus. It was at that moment I'd wanted to pick her up, swing her around and hug her forever. Jesus had given my sister back to me. Jesus, the One who'd known all along how this would end. At that moment, I felt the heaviness leave me. I felt light on my feet—free! Thursday April 6th will always be the happiest day of my life. Jesus gave me back my precious sister.

In retrospect- let me explain why I've entitled this story: Wake up Call:

In our lifetime, just how many lessons on life and loving are we shown- how many sink in- how many stay with us? If there were a message my Jesus has branded on my soul it is this: petty disagreements, inconveniences, all those bits and pieces that form stressful situations, are insignificant. What really matters is people, relationships, the love of each other, the caring arms and soothing words of a friend. A card arrived a few days after my return home. The person had written, "The children are praying too—and you know how powerful children's prayers are."

It is those acts of kindness that give us purpose and worth. When I feel I am falling back into the mire and my peace is becoming entangled in life's daily trials, I pull myself up onto the mountaintop and affix my priorities again. Those daily trials and entanglements shrink to the ground.

But there is something else I have learned: the inscription that my daughter had written on our boat: "Carpe Diem." This phrase holds more depth than people know. It means 'seize the day' and its letters stand out as flashing neon lights to me, since all this has happened. Make the absolute most out of each day. Don't just think a kind thought about someone, tell them. Don't put off that letter or thank you. Seize with all your might each opportunity to show- to tell your loved ones that you love them. Don't wait; for we have no assurance of tomorrow- but a full garden of flowers to give to people today.

I pray with God's help, I can hold tightly to this revelation and pass it on to whoever will listen. Praise to Jesus for revealing to me the most painful yet most valuable lesson I will ever learn.

In conclusion, I would like to quote the words of William Penn: 'I expect to pass through this life but once. If, therefore, there be any kindness I can show, or any good thing I can do to any fellow being, let me do it now, as I shall not pass this way again."1

My Sister, Dawn and I- doing what we love to do best of all- selling antiques at the Orinoco Gold Rush Days.

My Mother's day gift from my son, Josh, making me a fabulous fire pit!

AN ARM'S LENGTH AWAY
June 19th 1995

—◁◠◠▷—

Tonight Greg and I visited a friend in the hospital. He is dying of cancer. He's in the final stages. He is jaundiced and in isolation (we had to wash our hands and keep everything else out of his room). He cannot talk because he has a tube going down his throat. His stomach is huge due to the tumor. He lives on morphine and his pain on a scale of 1 to 10 is an 8. His name is George and he will soon be with you, Sweet Jesus. I felt somewhat privileged to be an arm's length away from a person who is but an arm's length away from heaven. Then I thought about how uneven and ragged and unfair things are. The day was gorgeous, people are traveling, planning vacations, shopping at the sales, building new homes, and falling in love. While George is lying in a cancer ward, barely alive. Lord, I know you call the shots, but I don't see any purpose or reason for this. I don't understand, sweet Jesus, I don't understand.

MOM'S NUGGETS OF GOLD

(for daughter Jessica on her
High School graduation)

—◈—

1. Don't let anyone steal your dreams—follow your heart, no matter what.
2. Ignore the phone when having dinner as a family.
3. Fight hard to not let the world squash who you are.
4. Faith. What really defines Faith? To me real Faith is not just believing with all your heart that Jesus can perform the miracle or that He can answer your prayers. Real Faith is believing in Him even if He answers them a different way.
5. Always respond to an act of love shown to you.
6. Be a woman of your word. This is a rare quality not many have.

7. Remember your "ministry" is where you are at any God-given, God- ordained moment, so be ready to be called to serve.

8. Be ready to tell warm fuzzies to people. When you think them, follow through and SPEAK THEM!

9. Be discreet and cautious when you share your confidences and concerns. Don't spill them out to business associates and casual friends, even if it is in a church setting.

10. If you are so led by the Holy Spirit to do something kind for someone- do not wait until the perfect time or convince yourself you need to 'get to the store' to get something better! Act on the NOW of it- the things that are available to you now. If you know you should write someone- to cheer them- just write the 'cheer' note on plain paper or whatever- better to get it off quickly than to wait indefinitely until you get around to getting to the store. (remember, any act of kindness, no matter how small, Is better than no kindness at all.)

11. Be swift to get thank you cards off.

12. In life, many times the joy is more in the journey (the looking forward to) than in the destination.

JOSHISMS

—⁓—

(my son, Joshua) has been given the rare gift of light heartedness, able to look at life with a smile, a chuckle. He is able to see the humor in everyday living. He has earned the title of '(muscle acher)' because he's always making me laugh so hard that my belly muscles ache!

January, 1994- We had been talking about doing the deck, the basement, mini-van and Maui- when all of a sudden Josh said, "Mom, I think our ship has come in."

After having listened to WCCO for school closings (30 Degrees below zero with 57 degrees below zero wind chill—) but Minnetonka school district did not get mentioned. Josh calls out, "Mom, What's Dick Brayer's (the district's superintendent) number?"

February, 1993- Greg and I were vacationing in Hawaii- but at home things got bad— our daughters, Tami and Jess, had the flu. The house wreaked and was a pig sty—Josh said, "Mom and Dad are in paradise, but we are in hell!"

July, 1994- I was driving Josh and his friend, Randy, to some garage sales. We noticed a sign for one some distance from the actual sale, so we ventured forth and followed the signs. When we finally did get there, it was just a bunch of old junk. On the way home, we spotted the sign again. It read: GARAGE AND CRAFT SALE—to which Josh quickly replied, "I should change that sign to read: GARAGE AND CRAP SALE!"

Here's our son, Josh- the creater
of all those hilarious 'Joshisms'!

MORE JOSHISMS

——⁓⁓——

August, 1995- It had been a rotten day- I was already feeling homesick and anxious because oldest daughter, Tami, was leaving for college the following day. We had been in the car- seemed like for hours (Tami, Josh and myself)- even went to a computer office store. I drove into a fast food drive-through and then everyone decided they wanted to go in—but wouldn't you know—2 cars had pulled up behind me—so I proceeded to turn around and leave—I said, "This is so stupid- I feel so stupid."—to which Josh replied, "It's Tami's music, mom (country western) it was playing on the radio. It makes everything look stupid." I just began laughing in spite of myself. I love him so very much.

December 1996- Josh and I were talking about my dimples I want when he said, "We don't even have groceries or milk in the house and you want dimples!"

I had found some black Nike's for Josh for back to school. When he looked at them he didn't like them. They were just TOO black! When I pressed the point (they WERE a good price after all- just $39.90), he finally said, "Mom, if you want me to get those, I may as well paint my feet black and go to school."

APRIL 1997

I had rearranged the furniture in the foyer, now with the school desk and potpourri lamp, causing it to jut out right by the kitchen entrance. Josh said, "Mom, I think that is a bad place for that. Someone is going to come along and bump it. Oh no!"

MAY 1997

Josh had announced he needed a new mattress. I told him to call and find out how much it would cost for a double mattress. He said $70. I said he had to call to make sure, to which he replied, "Unless you want the cheapest; but when you bought Tami's (his sister), you said you bought the cheapest because she rarely sleeps in it. You're the kind of people that buy 'crap' and keeps it forever and never replaces it again." I laughed so hard!

FIRSTS AND LASTS
SEPTEMBER 7, 1992

———ᴗᴗᴗ———

Firsts and Lasts, each one at opposite ends of life's yardstick - but with one thing in common-Each one comes equipped with two pieces of luggage – past memories and tears. They both force us to travel backward in time to recall the when's and used to be's. Like a silent star that falls from the evening's summer sky, the tears fall as those recollections of pictures of the past seem but painful collections of misty yesterdays. They also carry a surprise gift; for hidden and neatly tucked away, to be found at precisely the needed moment, there grows a seedling for a much needed "First"! Firsts have a way of gently drying those tears, giving us hope and reminding us that spring will always follow winter.

Firsts and Lasts, each one at opposite ends of life.

I WISH I COULD HAVE KNOWN

I wish I could have known when it was:

The last time I would be changing you from a messy diaper

The last time I would be nursing you

The last time I would be feeding you

The last time I would be bathing you

The last time I would be holding you on my lap

The last time I would be carrying you

The last time I would be riding you on the back of my bike

The last time you would be listening to me read to you

The last time I would be comforting you from a bad dream

The past memories link your tomorrows. Past recollections touch tomorrow's uncharted dreams. I feel so blessed to be a part of your fast-paced, joy-filled, ever sparkling, always changing world. Love you!

Mom

A BETTER DEE

JULY 8, 1994

—ᴥ—

I strive to be a better Dee- a Dee like Jesus wants and has plans for me to be. But so many areas need revamping. Lord, it is time- you go into those rooms of my heart and clean them out thoroughly. Some rooms are quite clean, but others need a complete housecleaning. Rooms with titles on them that read: gossip, sharp tongue, impatience, mind games, and selfishness. Change those rooms to be rooms of wisdom, caretaker of your money, standing up in a kindly way for what I believe, thinking before opening up my mouth, forgiveness, sincerity. For all these and more, Lord please help me become the Dee you have planned for me to be.

WOMAN:

Highly developed, finely-tuned sensitivities.

—◦◦◦—

APRIL 1998: Spoken to Greg when he presented me with roses and said, "It's nothing." To which I replied, "What you don't realize is, "Nothing is everything"!

WALKING WITH JESUS

JULY 14, 1994

—⟨⟨⟨—

Walking with Jesus is like walking on the road through life with twists, curves, and bends, rose gardens, streams in the desert, and bouquets of fresh daisies and mums placed strategically before me along the way.

IT'S A STRANGE THING
NOVEMBER 16, 1994

———✦———

It's a strange thing about flowers. When one receives them as a gift, they become a possession of enduring and eternal worth. Let me explain- What category do flowers fall under? Material possessions—no, for they are far above and beyond earthly worth. True, their beauty is short lived, but their ethereal magnificence far outweighs all earthly possessions.

FOOD FOR THOUGHT

——⟋∿∿⟍——

T rue friendship comes when silence between 2 people is no longer awkward.

CLEANING HOUSE
AUGUST 29, 1995

—⸙—

Dearest Jesus- Well, remember Last week when I went through the house with a fine tooth comb- getting rid of all kinds of junk? Jessica and I cleaned out her closet- I basically unloaded the house of unneeded junk. Well, now I need to look inward. I want to houseclean the parts of me I don't want. Like my house, I want to get rid of unneeded junk that have accumulated too long. But unlike the house, I cannot do this task myself.

ARE THERE BICYCLES IN HEAVEN?
Sunday, Sept 3, 1995

—◦∞◦—

Today the family and I packed up our bikes and drove to Carver park- then went on a gorgeous bike trip on the trails. Jesus- I once again felt so close to You. The day was gorgeous. I passed a lake, silent and blue- milk weed pods, so restful and therapeutic. I kept wondering why I had not done this before. I WILL go again soon. Thank you for such beauty with the family- truly a heavenly time.

I LEAVE A BIT OF MYSELF
FRIDAY, MARCH 17, 1995

———•••———

After a heavenly Maui vacation with my 5 loves, I am homesick for not only Maui- but the family. I just cannot shift gears as smoothly as others do. My mind continues to send forth flash pictures of Maui events. When I visit a beautiful place, I leave a bit of myself. But I also add another dimension of myself having now owned that experience, memories and joys. So, I am less. . . yet I am more. It is strange. The Australian memories continue to run into the Maui memories- like the threads of a cloth- running into and through other fibers of the same garment. Nonetheless, I know that a part of Dee remains in Maui; for I do feel at home there. When I arrived, it was as if my emotions, my joy, and my peace had been on hold- like I had been holding my breath- and finally, now I could let it all out and breathe again!

WHY DON'T WE EVER LEARN?
July 18, 1996

—◈—

A friend just called to say a dear friend was rushed to the hospital last night with severe stomach pain. She is in intensive care. They at first thought she had a bleeding ulcer- now they say it is a 'mass.' She cannot have visitors.

I am so glad I called her that day in early June to clear the air. But more than that, why don't we ever learn to just respect, appreciate and love one another? We do not know what another day will bring. Lord, teach me through this to appreciate my loved ones and friends and not judge them, ridicule or gossip- but to love them as You have taught us to do.

THE GRAPHIC LESSON
July, 1996

I recall, some years ago, that none of our children ever wanted to sit in the "very back" of our Oldsmobile station wagon, especially not in the hot summer months. Greg and I always told them not to complain—we assumed it simply could not be THAT horrible! Until one hot summer day, I sat back there. I was uncomfortably hot and smelled exhaust (gas fumes). I then understood. Today, I happened to lay down on my son's box spring in his bedroom (he'd moved his mattress to his college apartment.). I was horribly uncomfortable—and he had never complained. That did it. I went out and bought him a new mattress. Lesson learned for the day: DON'T JUDGE ANYONE UNTIL YOU HAVE SLEPT ON THEIR MATTRESS OR SAT IN THE BACK OF THEIR STATION WAGON!

ON GOSSIP-BEWARE:

———◦∾◦———

Gossip comes to us in various disguises, all appearing quite innocent at the time.

When someone is engaging in gossip with you, squelch it by saying something good about that person.

"Don't talk about your neighbors behind their backs. No slander or gossip please." Proverbs 24: 28 The Message Bible

A spouse may lure, invite, attract, welcome, and seduce one's mate, but NEVER CRITICIZE!

SPECIAL PHRASES THAT SAY MUCH

—⚬⚬⚬—

1. Perfect in their own imperfection.

2. There is beauty in the rawness of a true surprise on someone. For example: My husband surprised me with a romantic time of juice, crackers, cheese, rolls, card, candles, "I love you" balloons, cozy table and doilies in our bedroom. I had no idea what the surprise was, so I entered wearing my ugly pajamas and an old pink robe… proof that I really did not know about the surprise.

3. Some phrases, though trite sounding, can be very deep and from the heart. For example: I told my future son in law: "I am not losing a daughter; I am gaining a son."

4. "Immediate Friends"- meaning very soon we became close.

5. "On the Verge of Happiness." (Feb. 26, 1997) It was the eve of our trip to Maui and my daughter had come home to check out some wedding photographers. Remembering she had also been home when we had left for Guatemala

that snowy Sunday morning in March, I said, "You always seem to be here when I am on the verge of happiness."

6. Recollections are so important for they form a dot-to-dot pattern in the sequence of our life.

THOUGHTS IN PREPARATION
OF MY CHILD GETTING MARRIED
IN 3 WEEKS
Wed. July 16, 1997

—〰—

My Dear One,

The mixed emotions run rampant as I try desperately to maintain some level-headedness among all the tears, panic attacks and reminiscing. I use the analogy of transition in childbirth, when I had thought to myself, "This is way over my threshold of pain—way over!" The gripping truth remains: From the day my oldest daughter was born, I began working my way out of a job, "If I do it right." Yes, the years have flown by. Yes, I can see flashbacks of her and feel warm memories surround me and yes, I will probably ache inside as tears well up and spill over on August 9th. I want to feel and that is what I am doing. Feeling hurts. It rips, cuts, and bleeds. However, feeling also allows the passions and joys of all that life has to offer us, and that is exactly what living is all about. So as that day approaches, Jesus please let me sparkle and glow with love for my girl, and give me inward courage to graciously let go. There is beauty in that, as well: hurting, crying, smiling, laughing, feeling—*life*—and the harder I try to grasp it, the more it fades and disappears from sight. Seizing the moments (those precious moments) reminds me of the bubbles I blow for a young child, that pop so quickly. I can hardly remember they were there at all, and so it goes: seize, grasp, hold on, let go. Repeat. Life, you ARE quite beautiful!

THE MIRACLE

—◦◦◦—

I will always remember that day. My daughter and I were in the middle of tending to our garage sale. I noticed my daughter talking on her phone, saying scary words, 'You do not, you do not, I cannot believe this.' I then walked over to her and asked, "Who are you talking to?" To this she replied, 'Mom, sit down.' I wanted to know, but didn't want to know. Torn between blissful ignorance and reality, I looked at her and waited. 'Judy has breast cancer.' At that moment, my world, as I knew it, began spinning, tumbling, and crumbling all at the same moment. All I wanted to do is to get to her. I remember looking at my sale and thinking, "Dumb, everything looks dumb and pale to what is before us." From that point on, the day flew, as the neighbor took the sale, and I rushed to be with my girl. That evening a group of prayer warriors joined us in her family room for intense calling out to God for healing. Prophetic words were spoken and a resurgence of faith grew up that evening. Throughout her difficult chemo treatments, prayer vigils were being held as well as a powerful healing night at our home. Words of promised healing were spoken and believed upon. Eventually, her treatments came to a close and surgery loomed. Upon completion of extensive surgery, we all trusted our Jesus for the promised healing. It came. When she returned to the Mayo Clinic to be checked, they were so shocked by her "clean bill of health" that they had to go back in her records to see if this was even possible. I have seen the faith of both my daughter-in-law and my son. Their believing faith did , indeed, move mountains! Praise God for His never-ending faithfulness to our family. "For assuredly, I say to you, if you have faith as a mustard seed, you will say to this mountain 'move from here to there, and it will move and nothing will be impossible for you.'" (Matt. 17:20 NKJV)

THE CHALLENGE

July 5, 1998 (this was read to the family at a picnic gathering)

—◦◦◦—

Lately I have been thinking about relationships-from the fast-paced hello-goodbye kind, all the way to the soul mate, kindred spirit ones. I have watched my own children's love for their mates grow from the friendship of getting to know one another to a very strong, firm and flourishing life. I have watched my own friendships change as well. To me, friendships and family are everything. Nurturing, watering, feeding, and fertilizing are all the essential ingredients needed if the heartbeat of friendships is to remain steady and healthy. So, I began to wonder what marriages and relationships would look like if we were told that this would be our last day of life on this planet. Think how much more attentively we would listen to our loved ones as they spoke to us. Think how much more vivid and bright colors would look to us- they would be more like neon signs lighting up the night sky. All our senses would be sharpened and life and love would become electrifying. Perhaps our relationship with our Lord would even be more penetrating, sincere and intense.

Today, I would like to invite all of you to the challenge. For one week- each day you wake, imagine it is *your* last day: your last day to laugh, to cry, to feel. It's your last chance to know for certain that the people you love *know* that you love them. I hope you will consider this challenge. I think we would all be surprised at the results.

THE NOW OF MY LIFE

—⁓—

Yesterday, August 26th 1998, I was sitting on a picnic table bench at the Glen Lake Dairy Queen with my 3 year old daughter, Faith. I was enjoying the moment as we sat and drank our raspberry slush. I bitter-sweetly thought, "Someday I will return to this place after many years and reminisce how we used to. . .and I will say things like, "I would give anything to have those days back." But I AM in those days NOW- and my eyes widen- my appreciation deepens and my senses are sharpened as I grasp Faith, kiss her gently and tell her I love her. Lord keep me awake to the NOW of my life.

"Life should not ever be a contest. It should be looked on as a journey." (Dee)

"All of a sudden life appears to be traveling at too fast a speed. It is not that I want to say, "STOP, I want to get off"—But, instead,

I want to say, "Slow down, please, and let me enjoy the ride and smell those flowers". (Dee)

IN MEMORY OF AN EARTHLY ANGEL- WHO LEFT TO BE WITH JESUS THE EVENING OF JUNE 17TH, 1999.

—◦◦◦—

Y ou were here but for a fleeting few short moments in time- here to be a constant supportive, and loving companion to your husband; here to bring to this world three lovely children that you nurtured with a most Godly love and gentleness; here to spread the love of Jesus to a hurting and thirsty world; here to be a friend to so many people who were blessed to know you. Then, as if the music were turned off in the middle of the song, you left. No—you returned to your Master—the Master whom you most fervently served with all of your heart, mind, and soul. You have received your crown—you walk beside still waters and gaze into the very eyes of your Lord and Master. You have run the race and finished the course laid out for you. Praise God, you are HOME FREE!

LOVELY THOUGHTS

A n acquaintance or friend listens to what you say
But

A best friend listens to what you do not say.

Gracious speech is like clover honey—good taste to the soul, quick energy for the body. Prov. 16:24 The Message Bible

A TRIBUTE TO ALL THE PEOPLE
WHO HAVE MADE ME LAUGH)

Joseph (my precious dad)

Christopher (my oldest son).

Josh (my youngest son)

Dawn (my sister)

Joe (my son's father in law)

Tami (my daughter)

Jessica (my daughter)

Diane (my friend)

Faith (my daughter)

Greg (my husband)

LAUGHTER IS GOOD MEDICINE

—◦◦◦—

W hen I am asked what my hobbies are- I am always tempted to say: "laugh"! You see if there is one thing I love to do, it is laugh. No, I am not talking about the chuckle kind. I am talking about the REAL DEAL HERE! See, there is the quickie big smile cutsie kind; but what I am referring to is the kind of laughter that puts you out of commission for a time. It is the kind that lives on long after the event has occurred. I return to the daily swing of life. Then out of nowhere, I am reminded of that funny thing; and I once again am carried away in my euphoric love. I can recall attending the Chanhassen Dinner Theater with my sister. As we sat up close to the stage, all of a sudden I got this lame-brained thought and I wanted to share it with her. But every time I would open my mouth to tell her, I would begin laughing and could not get it out. Then there was this random story of my youngest son reliving a moment of his childhood- when he recollected my saying, "The mattress is SHOT!" Joe's account of waiting to go on a boat ride with his wife, who could not find her chapstick- pretty much sent me into laughter heaven as well.

So thank you to all the funny people of my world who continue to bless me with my favorite hobby!

"A cheerful heart brings a smile to your face; a sad heart makes it hard to get through the day." Proverbs 15:13 The Message Bible

A SUMMER'S MORNING-
A QUARTER TO 5 AM

Have you ever been out in the morning?
A quarter to five to be sure
Smelled the air,
Felt the breeze softly blowing
And gazed at the sky and its hues?
There's a soft whisper of rainbows
And the sound of bird's symphonies
Have you ever been out in the morning
A quarter to five if you please

Have you ever noticed each morning
How God's perfect plan for the day
Seems to blanket the earth in its splendor
And calls me to walk in His Ways

Have you ever felt with each morning
The feeling of newness and peace?
To begin with a song, feel His love-sing along
And with your burdens release
Have you ever been out in the morning?

If you haven't
Then now is the time
Take some moments of your day-
Feel the stress slip away
And welcome God's own Son-shine!

Have you ever been out in the morning
A quarter to five to be sure
Smelled the air, felt the breeze softly blowing
And gazed at the sky and its hues

There's a soft whisper of rainbows
And the sound of bird's symphonies
Have you ever been out in the morning
A quarter to five if you please.

(Written on July 7, 2001- my sister's arrival from Wisconsin- we'd gone outside to see her new car-me in my white nightie and robe—and oh what a morning!

THE TIME MAN

———〰———

I am now convinced that there exists this little 'time man' that sits around and watches to observe if anyone on this planet is having too much fun; and if he spots one- he magically fixes time to move twice as fast. That is why you always hear people say, "The time went so fast, it seemed more like 2 hrs, rather than 5 ½ hours!" He is also busy with s-l-o-w days- like listening to a monotone speaker or waiting for the pot to boil or ice cream to freeze. Then he lengthens the time because he knows we are impatiently waiting.

I love this word I just made up; "Foreverness"

GOD SIGHTINGS

———

It was Nov 30th, 2006. I was teaching at my pre-school when one of my more challenging boys began to cry. I really needed to work on those Christmas projects and was feeling stressed about getting it done. When clear as daylight, I heard the Lord say, "Hold him Dee, don't worry about the project- this is the most important thing you will do all day." So I helped him onto my lap. I felt like heaven was watching!

There are 3 ingredients needed in a home for a successful and healthy child, even though the home life may be dysfunctional.

1.Prayer 2. Affection 3. Laughter

If God has given you drums, play them. Whatever COLORS GOD HAS GIVEN YOU-WEAR THEM. THE SONG THAT GOD HAS GIVEN YOU-SING IT. WALK YOUR JOURNEY, SPEAK FROM YOUR HEART, AND SERVE THE KING OF KINGS!

There is not one prayer that does not get acknowledged and dealt with by our Jesus.

Remember, never feel awkward or uncomfortable if you feel you need to lovingly correct a person of high honor (pastor, preacher, missionary, etc.) "The ground is level at the foot of the cross."

We need to take more time to see the many ways the Lord's fingerprints are on our days.

WHEN TWO GOD-GIVEN GIFTS COLLIDE

——∿——

What happens when two God-given gifts collide? Today they did just that.

I was shopping at Joanne Fabrics and could hear this clerk (a very precious older woman) talking so sweetly and vivaciously to each customer as she checked them out. The customers were quite robotic and thought nothing of her. When it came time for her to help me, I looked at her and said, "You love people." She laughed and said she'd retired 4 different times and always returns because she loves people. I told her she returns because she is only happy when she is using the gifts the Lord has given her. She said, "You know I suppose that is right. I never thought of that." She thanked me and said, "God bless you." As I got into my car, I thought about my gift- the gift of encouragement, and her gift—loving on people. I had encouraged her at her loving people. Two gifts colliding-I had touched a bit of eternity today.

MORE OF YOU JESUS

—⚬⚭⚬—

The analogy of wanting more of what Jesus has to give us has been likened to walking into a large home- and being content to remain in the foyer——or getting on an elevator and getting off on the first floor, instead of going all the way to the top!

1 Thes. 5:19A The Message Bible

"Don't suppress the spirit"

GLIMPSES OF HEAVEN
Friday night, Jan 11, 2008

—◁∂∂▷—

I had tucked my grandson, Josiah, into his little bed. I bent down on my knees- clutched his little face in my hands and said, "Granma loves you very much, Josiah"- to which he replied in a most angelic sweet tiny voice (3 years old)- "I love you too Grandma."

THE GENERAL STORE

Jan 18, 2008

I love to stroll through this store, most appropriately known as "The General Store". It is most definitely a "woman's store" and has everything from hot cocoa to sweaters, monogrammed cookie jars to licorice. Today, as I walked through the aisles, I recalled how my precious mother loved this store. Every year she would say, "Next year, I will have more money—then I can buy some things." My eyes just filled with tears. How I wished I had asked her, "What is it you want?" I wished I had bought it on the spot because that "next year" did not happen for us.

I LOVE SATURDAY MORNINGS

Dec 8, 2007

—⚭—

I love Saturday mornings- today I watched the sunrise and Jesus told me He was glad I liked it. Isn't it sad that few people take time to pause and stare at the beauty He creates for us? People are so driven to go go go—not to pause and take it all in. Today will be fun. We have December errands. The sun is out and there is lots of snow and it's very cold, but we are a family. I love Saturday mornings.

Every now and then God shows us peek holes, behind the scene coverage on what the spiritual realm is busy doing. It is those times when God shines His headlights onto what has been going on all along - 'just behind the scenes'- and we see that things are clicking away for our good, on our behalf- if we make Him our priority.

BLACK AND WHITE PEOPLE/
BLACK AND WHITE TV

———⁓⁓⁓———

I remember watching black and white TV when it was quite new to the public. There I would be, sitting in front of it watching shows like Howdy-Doody, The Mickey Mouse Club, Flipper and Gilligan's Island. Then color TV was introduced. I saw it for the first time when I went with my dad visiting some of his landscaping customers. The peacock never looked so colorful. From then on, I was sold on color TV and soon my mom bought us our first console color TV.

Sometimes when I see various people, they remind me of our old black and white TV. There is no life, no passion, no flare, no vitality, drive, emotions or zest. Their faces appear expressionless- void of life. There is no peacock in sight!

TO BE LOVED ALONE
June 16, 2008

—⁓—

How deep the longing- how rare the opportunity. As I look back, the times are fleeting- more like a whirlwind experience- instead of a lazy summer's day remembrance.

This last mother's day, I was given a gift of all gifts. Because time is my strongest love language, this gift spoke volumes to me of love. I had been handed a Mother's Day card by my son, Josh. In it, he had written that for my gift he would come over after work and the 2 of us would get my perennial garden back in shape. Soon after I'd received this card, I got a call from him and we set a date. We talked as we pulled weeds; and he dug a trench-type border all around- then laid beautiful black bark on top. There we were, me in my big straw hat and garden gloves- and poor Josh sneezing and scratching his throat like crazy. But never once did he complain. Never missing a beat, he worked, ignoring his allergies. The day was perfect- blue skies- gentle breeze and no interruptions. I recall looking up to thank my Jesus. Then all of a sudden it hit me. I looked at him and asked (not really meaning it to be a question), "Josh, when was the last time we were together alone?" We both were silent.

All too soon those moments had ended. What had been 2 ½ hours seemed like 15 minutes. But all that says is that our time together was so meaningful and cherished that time had stood still for us. Now, a week later, if you were to ask me what we talked about, I would hardly remember. The important thing is that we "loved alone."

JUST ONE MORE DAY

August, 2008

—⦿—

S eems every special moment in time is shy one day of feeling complete. My sister had been here visiting. I had assumed she was leaving on Sunday; but. had so wished for 'just one more day' with her. I learned a few hours later, that they were leaving to go back on Monday. On this occasion, I was able to get my last day- a rare exception.

Now that 'one more day' syndrome extends to specialized days as well. If it is a day that I need more hours, It is a feeling of incompleteness (like leaving out an ingredient in a cookie recipe), or an unfinished sentence. Perhaps, someday I will feel like I have squeezed every drop of juice from the orange, and scraped every ounce of cake batter from the mixing bowl—I just want to feel like that moment is complete. Jim Croce said it best with his song: "Time in a Bottle."

THE SERENDIPITY

———*ᴧᴧ*———

T hey are fun. I mean even the word sounds fun. I love saying it. There I am commenting on how pretty a little girl looks for her pre-school graduation—when the mom says, "Like *Fancy Nancy.*" She asks if I have heard of those books. I reply that I have not; but within a few hours, I am thumbing through some books at a garage sale and there's one of the books: *Fancy Nancy*!

THE AWAKENING
June 16, 2008

—✦—

Today I feel like a layer of skin is being peeled away. God is speaking to me—an empty flask being poured into. I am crying. It is 9:49 AM on a Monday morning and the tears come in, then go out, patterned like the tide. I feel God speaking. "Stop striving, only be real, be you. You cannot take on the whole world. It is okay to say no sometimes. Don't be afraid to speak truth into people's lives; don't be afraid to tell people your opinion, if asked. (Sometimes even if not asked.) It's okay to disagree. You must be true to yourself. Take time to just back away and be quiet, to think, to allow the luxury of silence, and to be okay among friends. Learn to really listen and don't be afraid to ask questions if you don't understand what has been said. Give people grace. Never allow yourself to become bitter. Never feign emotions; check your motives. Always come up alongside of your husband during good and bad times; be there for him.

Never ever gossip, it is like spitting garbage. Take the focus off of you, and if it is not on you, keep it that way. If there is a time for the focus to be on you, then I, Jesus, will turn the floodlight on you. It is never your job to do that—it is God's job. Be free to do, free to joke, to laugh, to be goofy, and to cry (without apologies). Wave the colors of your flag!"

Jesus wants me to know that 'all sides' make up the me that I am. When that side known as depression rears its head, praise music lifts my soul and chases out those demons. There is no room for pretense or phony words. Call a spade a spade; just remember to say it with love—for that is the hidden and difficult key- to learn to say difficult things in love—not aggressively, but softly with clarification. Remember to thank people. Remember to thank God. Pray in details—thank in details. Don't lose your temper—for if you do, you will have regrets. Words hurt—keep in control, even if you must walk away. Stay in control.

Learn to trust the God who made you- call upon Him at any time. Listen harder to His voice and take it to heart. Don't ever hold back from blessing someone, whether it be with a kindness done or a word said. Just do it—never ever put it off—do it now! Go with your gut—(they are little cues from God- learn to receive them and act on them). Learn to listen with your heart—but also your head. (Don't be gullible.)

I feel like my soul has been drenched in a refreshing stream of crystal water—I come up from the fountain—I have been renewed, and refreshed. I will begin my day. "He has put a new song in my mouth. Praise to our God; many will see it and fear, and will trust in the Lord." (Ps. 40:3 NKJV).

THOSE CELLAR SIDE-LINERS
(Aug. 19, 2008)

Another gorgeous morning 6:30 AM. My two daughters and I are on our Tuesday morning two-mile run. I am feeling great and full of good energy. Along the way I meet up with an older man walking in the opposite direction, aggressively preaching to me that running is hard on the body. He says walking is better; "don't work so hard!" Blah, blah, blah, blah. I continued on with my run, patronizingly answering him, "I know, I know." Yet, I could not help but see a crystal clear analogy come floating to the surface. Isn't it just like life that when you begin a dream or conquest and your focus is on the target, there will always be a few that drag you down with discouraging words? I continued the run, right past the man; so in life we run on, keeping our eyes on the prize!

GOSSIP- ALL DRESSED UP IN CHRISTIAN STYLE

August 20, 2008

—◦◦◦—

Today I experienced a display of what I call "Christian Gossip". Oh I know it is all evil- but I am not so sure we always recognize all of it as just that. Here's how it can go: "Oh I am going to ask _____ to volunteer at church to help teach. I do hope she's feeling better. You know she is on those anti-depressants, gained a lot of weight and her husband said she lays in bed all day." What you have read is a rendition of a Christian seemingly concerned about a church member, but giving out way too much info! It happens to us all, but watching this performance before my very eyes showed me the gross hypocrisy of our Christian ways. The main tragedy here is that most of the time this sin goes unrecognized. Lord, give us eyes to see the character assassination we construct when we gossip, "All dressed up in Christian style."

"Listening to gossip is like eating cheap candy; do you really want junk like that in your belly?" Proverbs 18:6–8. The Message Bible

WHEN GOD ANSWERS PRAYERS

L ast night our first born and his girl friend surprised us with the news—they are engaged! I have never ever seen them happier. It is something that I have been praying for in my son's life for many years. I recall her first week-end with us- we had family prayer- and I spilled out my heart to her- telling her how very blessed I was that God had heard our cries and had sent someone special into our son's life—(of course the family was embarrassed for me and thought my assumptions and candidness would scare her off). Now, 3 ½ years later- they announce the news- Proof (as if we need it) that He does hear our prayers- always in His timing!

ON FATHERHOOD TO MY FAMILY
(Sunday, June 15, 2008)

—⟨∿∿⟩—

For the fathers of today, for the fathers of tomorrow—First I just want you to know how very much you are respected, honored, needed, leaned on, cried on and blessed. To a Godly man- being a father is not just a title of bread-winner or superiority in the home. It is so very much more. A father, one who runs his home under the umbrella of Jesus, is anointed by God to be the mantle by which the entire family feels cared for, protected and loved. It is that feeling inside that whispers, "Daddy's home, now everything is going to be alright." I watched the love flow beyond measure as my son in law gets down on the floor with his children and plays with every ounce of his spirit- and every bone in his body. I have seen steadiness like a rock when the pressure mounts to unbelievable portions and yet- he peacefully quiets the storms. I have witnessed his quiet times, when he replenishes his supply from the God he loves with all of his heart- Matt, Happy Father's Day- you wear that honored title so well. I love you.

TO CHRIS:

I always get teary-eyed as I imagine you as a father- actually my eyes are welling up even as I write this. For, my dear son, you will bring to this child so much of what you yourself are- you will someday soon be able to join forces with your sweet Jesus in loving, molding,—sweetly and gently pointing that child to the feet of our Lord; and you, Chris, will do that oh so lovingly and gently. What a gift to your children you will be.

TO JOSH:

Oh the laughter that will grow in your home- like a basket of glitter that sprinkles from above- so will be the joy and antics of your fathering. To you, my dear son, the glass will always be half-full; there is always a rainbow after a storm, and joy will forever follow sorrow. Your children will catch that- and the world will be a brighter place because there will be more of your spirit in your children.

TO MY HUSBAND, THE FATHER OF 5

—◦◦◦—

Y ou have weathered the turbulent storms, basked in the glory of your dedication to your family and taught them oh so much. They have learned from you that it is a good thing to work hard- that hard work pays off- but that there is a time to enjoy life as well- to joke, to laugh, to be real; You have taught them what to do when the storm rages and the forest seems oh so dark. You are ever so quick to give all the glory to your Lord for your blessings- and your children have seen a father who has faithfully taken time to discipline—never in anger- always calm, following through with time and tenderness after the spanking. He has now qualified you to carry a bigger staff; and I have already seen you pick it up. My husband- daddy of 5- grand daddy of 7 and counting. That bigger staff looks so good on you- I applaud you for all that you are- as my husband, our children's father- and patriarch of the family. You are loved and needed mightily!

TO GUARD YOUR HEART

(Sept. 2008)

—⟡—

It was our Washington D.C. trip. Chaperoning this trip with my daughter Faith had proved to be more challenging than anticipated. As we came walking a couple yards from the hotel's lobby, I was approached by a young woman in extreme despair. Trembling and crying, she told us she just found out her mom had been in a terrible car accident and she had no way of getting home. She asked if I could loan her money. She said that she would pay me back tomorrow, that she worked in the sports store at this mall. She said she would get the money to me. As I handed her the $45, I said, "I give you this in the name of Jesus." She then grabbed the money and asked me to pray for her mom. I laid my hands on her and prayed, first for the peace for the young woman, and then for her mom. She then was gone. The following day, my mind continued to return to the woman and my money. That evening, upon returning to the hotel, I made one focused dash to the front desk, only to learn that no envelope had been placed there for me. We then stopped at all four sports stores, describing her and asking if she worked there. When we'd finally entered the final fitness store, I was ushered to the owner's office and was pointedly told that they were sorry this happened to me, but that I would never see even $1 of that money ever again. After many tears, I reported it to the security guard and police at the hotel, only to be told by the police that this is what these people do—they make a living doing this—and that they cannot be arrested because people give them money willingly. I felt abused, used, and stupid. What hurt the most was that this woman had taken advantage of one of my strongest gifts: compassion. Two very strong positives were raised out of all the muck. 1. I had prayed for her- and Jesus had promised that His word would never return to Him void. 2. What is the lesson here that my Lord is teaching me? My daughter put it quite succinctly: He wants me to guard the gifts He has given to me. Just as a prostitute gives herself to everyone because she does not feel she is of value, I too had freely given my compassionate spirit away. The Lord does not want me to do that; He needs me to act with prudence and wisdom. I need to guard this gifting, for it is gold to be given out with caution and grace. It was a most painful lesson taught, yet very much worth it. Lord, help me to have learned this truth.

WORDS OF PEARL

(Sept. 2008)

When He speaks new assignments, there will always be new lessons for new growth.

Today He told me I need to forgive those who do not forgive me.

New life comes out of dark places

DESCRIPTION OF AUTUMN

—◦∾◦—

"Enjoy the beauty of fall as the glory of the Creator God shines through the harmony of a multitude of colors."

THE LAST ROSE OF SUMMER AND THE ROSE BUD OF HOPE

—◦◦◦—

It was October and once again I was winterizing my flower garden- the yearly job of cutting down all the summer flowers that had long since blossomed and faded. As I clipped away, I began to think how sweet it would be to find 'a last rose of summer' amidst all the dried blossoms. Seconds later, quietly hidden behind a Hydrangea leaf, I spotted this gorgeous pink beauty- a rose in all her splendor (perfect as can be)- My last rose of summer. I began to cry and thanked the Lord for His continual reminder of His ever presence in my life. My eye was then drawn to yet another of His miracles- a rose bud (not yet opened). It reminded me of hope- for though winter is fast approaching, a rose bud is a reminder to me of the promised blossoming of still more of His Glories yet to come in my life here.

THE LETTING GO

———✎✎———

She held out a ribbon that had been used to tie her birthday bag. "It's like this," she gently yet firmly explained. "If they ask you for more space, don't hold on tightly but instead give them another inch . (at that she completely released the ribbon from her hands) Give them all–and if you can do this, I promise it will return to you 1000 fold!"

She is my advice queen—and I am deeply grateful to her words of gold—she is beautiful and she is my daughter.

"Earth is crammed with heaven and every common bush afire with God, but only those who see take off their shoes, the rest sit round it and pluck blackberries and daub their natural faces unaware."

Elizabeth Barrett Browning

HIGHLIGHTS OF CHILDHOOD
AND HOW EVERYTHING
IS MAKING SENSE
(Oct. 2008)

———⟡———

I really don't know exactly what brought the thoughts on, but I began looking back on my life and all the major events that formed the skeletal structure of what I call my past. I began to see a plan—*the* plan—, like stepping stones around flowerbeds, deep dark forests, rushing water falls, fields of lilies, still waters, and raging storms. The stepping stones continue, all pre-laid by the One who travels with me. It all makes total sense. He is using all the pain and tears to grow and stretch me.

He doesn't cause the pain, but He uses it very well.

I began thinking about childhood memories. Here are a few I can recall: being picked up every Friday from my grade school by my mom and dad so we could go to Waukesha and do our big weekly grocery shopping.

Walking down Calhoun Road with my mom and sister to Calvary Lutheran Church on Sundays. Dad would join us later to usher.

Returning home from school Wednesday afternoons; the smell of newly baked warm cinnamon rolls met me as I climbed the stairs and the newly dusted and vacuumed upstairs farmhouse flat where we lived sparkled.

Sunday afternoons were always chicken dinners served in our warm and humble dining room.

I remember sea foam candy and mom's homemade fudge. She'd stir it fast, then show me how to take a spoonful and let it hang, forming strings. She'd say, "When it forms into 1 complete unbroken string, it is ready." Sometimes she would test it on a plate.

Dad would always bring our dog, Rusty, in at night. He'd be tied up outside all day and mom would say, "Joe, go get Rusty."

I remember Mom sitting at her old blond desk, reading from her little white Bible. Dad, after working a long day as a landscaper, eating his supper on his tray and watching TV.

My grandma, Mema, lived in the downstairs flat of the farm house. She would call up the stairs, "Florence, Florence." (my mom's name). Then she'd give mom one of her home-baked goodies. It was usually her awesome rhubarb kuchen, with warm icing dripping down the sides.

Driving to school in our Model T with the hole in the floor. Oh, how I hated going. I was so terribly homesick.

The two of us (mom and myself) would have our own devotions from the little Lutheran devotional book while I lay in bed each evening.

Riding our bikes (mom and me)- with my little sister, Dawn, sitting on the back bumper of my bike with a pillow under her, to get our hair cut in the little town of Brookfield.

Swimming at the Greenfield pool with my best friend and cousin, Julie.

Being paid $2.00 for raking the leaves and trimming the hedges for Grandmother Mema.

Playing house, building leaf forts, and riding our tricycles with my buddy, Julie.

Sleeping over in cousin Julie's big tent and her brother scaring us.

Playing Monopoly with my cousins Julie and Dan. (I always lost and ran home crying).

Playing with catalog cutouts with cousin Julie on the living room rug and building blanket forts in the living room. (Wow, mom was a saint to let us do this.)

Cousin Julie and I dressing up in our mom's evening gowns and walking around the yard singing songs by the Everly Brothers and Dodie Stevens. (our moms were professional singers).

My childhood friend and cousin, Julie,- we grew up together since we were 2!

My Daddy and Me—just loving on him- I was such a 'Daddy's girl!

Me as a little girl posing with my sweet mom.

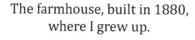

The farmhouse, built in 1880, where I grew up.

THE BATTLE BELONGS
TO THE LORD

—⚬⚬⚬—

After an extremely difficult emotionally draining day, with the battle raging all around, I suddenly felt the victory—and as I prayed, I said, "It's over." I could feel the demons running- and God's army standing in victory. Oh it is true alright- there is a host of angels leading us on to victory.

AGAINST PRINCIPALITIES AND POWERS AND STRONGHOLDS
Nov 10, 2008

———⟨⟨⟩⟩———

I t had been rough- battling wars is always tough- leaving the warrior weak, weepy and frail. But if done right, with spiritual eyes, the wars can be won with no casualties- just a great deal of clean-up.

My daughter looked at me with eyes of deep love and stated most assertively: "Mom, you are fighting for future generations." I pondered that statement and the following day received insight into just exactly what it meant- Strongholds in my life- the heavy expectations placed on people, (especially family members) Then there is the biggest one of all: conflict resolution. I knew nothing about it. I had once seen it done by an awesome family, but other than that, I had no role models in childhood or adulthood. So I'd learned how to fight from how I had watched it played out as a child. You fight with intense manipulation- you always aim for the heart- and you don't let up until your victim falls. The words are razor sharp and poisonous, with labels and accusations. That is how I fought—until now. I guess sometimes the Lord rises up an outsider to come in and blow up the entire dysfunctional strategy. When someone blows the whistle on strongholds, they lose their grip and the battle begins, because that is exactly what the word "stronghold" is. A stronghold does not acquiesce easily—the behavior has gone on too long and the victim that is in bondage will fight. Then, because of God's ever faithful mercies and grace—there is a breakthrough—and a tiny flicker of light and understanding can be seen. The processing comes next as one tries to understand the core of the hold. Caring friends serve as sounding boards and are probed with questions that so desperately need answers. For in that process, truths, enlightenment, and breakthrough are birthed. It came for me last night. As I placed question after question before Him- trying my hardest to make sense out of it all, He would answer directly, yet lovingly. Being a pre-school teacher- I have seen many children who actually have needed to be taught how to be a friend. I had previously believed that the ability to be and make friends came as a package deal at birth. As I experienced teaching, I had been faced with a truth: Not all children have a built in, home grown friendship factory. They actually need to be shown step by tedious step. That was me last night. As my husband actually walked me through the process of how to confront, I was able to see clearly all my stumbling blocks. With examples of "what to say" and "what not to say," I was learning valuable lessons and God was breaking the chains of generational strongholds in the process. It is morning now. How do I feel? First, I know the battle has been won. There's nothing left now but the cleanup. Create in me a clean heart oh God, and take not They Holy Spirit from me. Praise God, I am free. The wounded soldier grips the hand of her Shepherd and rises- we continue our walk together and I persevere. "For we do not wrestle against flesh and blood, but against principalities, against powers, against the ruler of the darkness of this age."

(Eph. 6:12 NKJV)

MORE THAN CONQUERORS
(Fri, Dec. 19 2008)

—◦◦◦—

"In all these things we are more than conquerors through Him who loved us." (Rom. 8:37 NKJV)

It is 5:16 am on Friday morning. It is now Dec. 19th. I was woken by the sad memory of what had just occurred a few hours earlier: My youngest daughter's Christmas program at her church school. She had lost hours of sleep over it. She had been honored with a special singing part. Many family members had attended—both big brothers and her sister in law, one of which had driven 1 ½ hours just to be there for her. As I lay in bed, reflecting on what had happened, I replayed the unfortunate incident. For no apparent reason, her microphone had ceased to work just before the program was to begin. So when her time had come to step up and sing her song, we could barely hear her. As I videoed her, I kept motioning with my left arm to pump up the sound, to no avail. I felt a wave of nausea on her behalf. Faith's expression screamed to me, "It's not working." She finished her song and sat down. After the program, I hugged her and saw intense disappointment written on her face, the likes of which I had never seen on her before. My girl rarely ever cries. Now she was nearly sobbing and ready to burst. Then she walked away from me. It was not until we returned home that I heard the "inside story" from God's journal. It goes as follows:

Minutes before the program had begun, Faith knew her microphone was not working, so she began praying earnestly. As she sat with her group, singing, she continued to pray for God to do His miracle and fix the microphone. When she'd stepped up to the front and center stage and began singing, it became apparent it was still broken. She knew, but still continued to sing. After the program, and after seeing me, she began her battle. Through her earthly eyes, she saw no weapons, yet she was battling against Satan himself. She heard his laughter, "I ruined your night; I took your voice away." But God said, "You did a good job." As she walked around the gym, she became fully aware of Satan's plan to bring her down low; but with everything in her, she fought her battle with all the strength of a warrior and decided to fight back- she resisted his most ferocious attacks and decided to go around and tell her fellow performers what a great job they had done. Through that act, God was able to smooth out the sharpness of the disappointment. My daughter had been given a life lesson from God- and had passed the test with flying colors- She had proven the Sword of the Spirit- the word of God- to be true. We can be more than conquerors- and on the evening of Dec. 18th, 2008- she became a champion!

But there is more to this open-mouthed story—for sometimes when it is imperative that God's plan is to teach us a life lesson, He softens the blow to the others and compassionately fills in the cracks. Let me explain: When her big sister announced on Tuesday that she would not be able to attend the evening performance, we'd mentioned to her that there is a dress rehearsal performance for the senior citizens on Wednesday afternoon. I had felt a strong urge to attend with her as well. As I made plans to meet them there, I heard a soft voice whisper, "This program today is more important than you know." As I sat watching, I felt saddened by the fact I had not come prepared with my camcorder. Oh well, I convinced myself, I have Thursday evening. The program went very well. My older daughter left with her children; and as I was walking out, I saw one of the dads who had come prepared, decked in camcorder attire. I'd mentioned to him that I'd wished I would have come prepared. He said he always comes, each year, on dress rehearsal day,—that way he can sit back and enjoy the evening performance. He said he would be happy to make a copy for me. I remember feeling humbled as I ventured forth with a whole- hearted, "Yes" and what would be the cost—His answer told me it was probably free. I drove home thinking that I will probably never get it and that 'talk is talk'. But, as my husband and I were sitting in our chairs- way early before the evening performance began, the father excitedly handed me Wednesday's video. I was astounded and quickly stood up and gave him a hug- thanking him over and over. But it wasn't until after the performance that I realized how very precious that tape was. So I ask you, was it just chance that Faith's big sister could not attend the Thursday night performance which had me also come on Wednesday? Was it just coincidence that I happened to leave the building on Wednesday afternoon and walk to my car the same time that this dad with the camcorder did?

We are always experiencing the raw reality of God's fingerprints in our lives in the details of our days—we just need eyes to see it.

THE RECOVERY
(Sept. 1, 2008)
(written to my husband, Greg)

—∿∿∿—

The prairie sunflower lies peacefully on the B & B dress-er—a visible reminder of yesterday. It whispers softly of a long walk on a beautifully wooded, peaceful trail, hand in hand, taking an occasional picture, then more walking. The weather is perfect. I see a birch tree—it calls to me of carved initials and love forevermore. You, without hesitation, begin the task at hand—sweating through it all. You carve the art piece precisely as such: G (heart) W-08—We attempt to arrange the camera just so for the picture—we miss—we laugh—we try again—we continue our walk. Then, as if on some romantic compulsive whim, you walk a few steps ahead and return to fumble with my hair. You place a prairie sunflower in amidst my wind-blown tresses— it was a moment in time that I could barely absorb.

These getaways are way more essential than our eyes can see and our heart can feel, for it is in these unobtrusive moments—whenever and wherever they come—that there is a feeling of recovery. Things appear to get lost in the shuffle of time. But in a moment I realize I was wrong, it was not lost. . . just a bit of a distance away. It is like a volleyball that gets served so haphazardly that one would almost dismiss it as a lost point, only to find that someone had recovered it and it is once again sent on its volleyball journey.

I see rekindling as recoveries—where old becomes new and the past turns into present. Even though that yellow flower now lies somewhat limp on the B & B dresser, the message whispers just as sweetly as first it was picked. One man, one woman, and a peaceful walk in the woods.

THE RECEPTIONIST/THE PARTY
(Jan 8, 2009)

---⟿---

I stepped into the waiting room and was immediately greeted by a perky woman, perhaps in her late 50's. I handed her my paperwork. She asked what I did. I told her I was a pre-school teacher. Her face lit up as she said that that would be a fun job. Then she walked me to my dressing room and proceeded to show me where to go after I was dressed in my smock. Upon completion of the procedure, I put my street clothes on and returned to her waiting room. She warmly told me to have fun with those little people. We chatted back and forth. I mentioned that she would love what I do as well, but that she had a powerful ministry right there. She looked up, as if I had given her a great compliment and said she had never had anyone describe her job quite like that before. I told her it truly was for her, because she did such an awesome job of it. She then mentioned all the hurting people that she tries to cheer up, but that she does encounter opposition. I then told her it was because she was doing God's work and satan does not like it. Then I told her that I knew she was a Christian. She looked at me and said, "You know, when I look into your eyes I see your very soul." Then she ran and got her "soul mate"—Rosey—an awesome woman who also loves Jesus. I hugged her and we all totally spirit-connected. It was a surreal feeling. As I proceeded to leave, I looked at them both and said, "Keep glowing." Then a patient who had been sitting in a chair waiting, stood up and said, with a big smile on her face: "She *is* glowing." We all laughed and felt His spirit envelop us in love and joy. As I left that office, I softly said, "Wow!" When I walked out of the building to my car, I heard my Jesus laugh, a real belly laugh. I guess He got blessed as well!

TEACHER SIT BY ME
(Jan 15, 2009)

———ɷɷ———

It has been 22 years now that I have taken up my post as a certified pre-school teacher. As I look back, I can see a mix of rough roads and smooth pathways—of storm clouds, harsh winds, sunshine, and soft warm breezes. But then there are the children bursting with love- that have passed through my door and my life- and have left a heart print etched on my spirit. I remember the little girl who hugged me all throughout the day- or the little boy that needed to know 'in advance' what we were doing next and next and next. The boy that God had told me to, "Just hold him." Then there are those children of compassion with caring ways and tender hearts. Like little angels, they give gentleness and love to me and their classmates. For but a very short time, each year, I am entrusted by God and their parents to love, nurture, hug, and teach these lambs. What do I want them to remember? Sure, it is great that I provide the educational

Stepping stones for their mental growth; but really I just want them to remember that they had fun with a teacher that loved them unconditionally and loves what she does. I have but a moment in time to show them what love means. Lord Jesus help me make each moment count.

Precious words spoken by my grandchild to her mom when it was suggested they return the gift I'd given her. With tears in her eyes she said, "No mommy, their gift has their love all over it."

SHELLY'S SHOWER
(Jan 17, 2009)

—⁓—

When we first began our home expansion, I had spoken of this event. I remember calling out to Jesus for Him to bring someone special for my precious son. Years traveled by, And then one day I'd received a phone call. My son was calling, saying that he and a woman named Michelle had spent a long time talking and he seems to feel very comfortable with her. They came and I prayed and thanked the Lord for her. Now, here I was preparing for her bridal shower. The home is ready. It rests peacefully, almost in anticipation of the joys that await her under this roof, the walls ready to absorb all the laughter, tears, and love it can hold. I have prayed over every chair and invited Jesus and His angels to join us. He said He would come. It is 11:45 and I am ready.

Our oldest son,
Christopher, wife Shelly
Girl, and grandsons
Liam and Maxwell

Our daughter, Tami,
husband Matt, and
grandchildren Rachel,
Josiah, Grace, and Ben.

Me sandwiched
between my fantastic
sons, Christopher
and Josh

SELF ANNIHILATION
(Feb 12, 2009)

—⟨⟩—

I drove right past a lost puppy, nervously walking in the middle of the road. I slammed the door in my husband's face. You know it is strange how this all works. I know when I go to Him, confess my sins, He forgives me and cleanses me- as far as the east is from the west- Still, I continue in my self condemning spidery web. Going back to the scene of the crime, I rehearse over and over again exactly where I was, what was said, and how I blew it. I never allowed His forgiveness to soak into the very fiber of my being. Still, He waits for me to come to terms with reality—a contrite heart—He loves so much and He says to me, "My Dee, I love you, and it is time now to put the mistakes of yesterday behind you. They are over—it is a new day—and I see your heart, pure because of Me. So live and rejoice in the newness of today. I love you, I love you, I love you!"

"Come now let us reason together," says the Lord, "Though your sins are like scarlet, they shall be a white as snow, Though they are red like crimson They shall be as wool" (Isa. 1:18 NKJV).

THE CONFERENCE
(Feb. 26, 2009)

—〰—

It had started out quite vanilla like- quite similar in style to most of my other conferences. I talked, she talked. I listened, she listened. . . and so it went. But just when I thought we were finished, things turned off from the beaten path and we found ourselves on a road much less traveled. She asked, "Do you find him sad and almost angry?" That question was the sharp turn that took us down this strange new road—which I now call, "God Time." I think what she really needed was validation on what she had seen in her son. Months earlier, I had thought the child difficult and somewhat scary. Now my suspicions were met head on with his mom's. I prayed for her. She cried. I hugged her and listened more. When she left, I was taken back by His finger-prints on this day. There had been no one signed up immediately after her- so we had been given a large chunk of time devoted just for her. As I got into my car and drove down the road, I was humbled that God had chosen me as His vessel to bring love, encouragement and understanding to a hurting mother. I have heard it said that God chooses particular people to get certain jobs done. If you refuse, He will find someone else, but you were asked first and it is you who will receive the blessing. Thank you Jesus that in the late Autumn or early Winter of my career, you have brought me to a new height, a new place to serve You.

DANDELIONS AND DIXIE CUPS-THE MAY DAY SURPRISE

(does it get any better?)

—⟨∾∾⟩—

I happened to be walking into my foyer when I saw them moving ever so quickly around my outside front door. I hid myself, hoping they had not seen me. It was then I heard an ever so gentle knock. I waited a few moments, allowing them time to scamper away. I then opened the front door- to find two small white plastic Dixie cups, each one holding the most popular children's flower God ever created, the dandelion. These small cups proudly boasted of dandelion bouquets. Two little white notes had been lovingly tied onto the top rim of the cup, together with hand drawn smiley faces. I looked and discovered them standing by the neighbor's tree (partly hidden)- yet oh so visible to me. I tenderly scooped up the cups then yelled, "Thank you! You made my day!" I walked inside and exclaimed, "Does it get any better than receiving dandelions in Dixie cups on May Day by angel granddaughters?" I answered the question, "No, it doesn't get any better!" Thank you for the flowers, Jesus.

TWO TURKEYS AND SOME DRUMSTICKS

We dream in literals (April, 2009)

—⟨∿∿⟩—

I had been feeling inadequate, dull, lifeless and stupid. That night I dreamed I had been asked to bake some food. I grabbed my chicken drumsticks and placed them in the oven. Minutes later, someone walked into the kitchen and commented on the delicious aroma wafting from the oven. I felt so proud of myself. Soon after, I removed the drumsticks from the oven. At the same time, someone walked in with two awesome butter-browned huge turkeys. Embarrassed, I quickly pushed my drumsticks aside. Now if that dream doesn't play out my inner feelings, nothing does!

MY NEW TWIN GRANDBABIES
May 28, 2009
MY HANGING BASKET NURSERY

—◦◦◦—

They are here, well, most of them. Our twin boys arrived on Thursday, May 14, 2009. Our baby birds that have been nestled in my hanging basket are mostly hatched as well. These helpless little bundles with scantly clad feathers and wobbly necks—any noise or movement and their mouths open like there's no tomorrow. A few days ago, I held the twins. I held their heads and talked to them, their little legs and eyes that sleep a great deal, their furrowed brows and new smooth skin. They are so new, Lord Jesus, new life in my hanging basket and new life in the Brown family.

THE HOUSE THAT I DRIVE BY
(May 28, 2009)

—◦◦◦—

I drive by a special house at least twice a day. I imagine all the love, laughter, tears and life that run through there each day. I glance at the swing set, a child's dream play yard. I can almost hear their playful laughter. I thank you Lord for this house that I drive by, for within its walls is a family of great strength and faith—a praying family—grounded and cemented in love. They are the family of my daughter and son in law and houses my four precious grandchildren. I will not allow myself to ever take this gift for granted. THIS SPECIAL HOUSE THAT I DRIVE BY!

THOSE PRE-PLANNED BLESSINGS
(June, 2009)

—ᴖᴖ—

D id you ever plan an event way ahead of time only to discover that when the event arrived, it was significantly more timely than you could have ever dreamed?

We had planned to go strawberry picking with Chris, way up in Clearwater (one hour away) on a lovely Saturday morning. Sadly, when the day finally arrived, serious family issues had me driving there alone. I had been quite lonely the day before and stressed over my problems. Little did I know God had seen this coming and so had this day pre-planned with a ribbon around it just for me.

First, I was blessed to spend the entire day with my son. We strawberry picked our hearts out, ate a pint of ice cream (with sliced strawberries toppling over), then drove to his house where I attempted to repair his car seats. We enjoyed supper together.

By the time I returned home, I felt renewed and refreshed. Thank you, Jesus, for planning that day's itinerary.

SUNSHINE ON MY SHOULDERS

—◦◦◦—

I t was Wednesday, January 27th, 2010. We Minnesotans were just barely coming out of a "five days of no sun" spell and I was feeling really down. The sunshine part of the day was that I had my two angelic grandbabies with me on the ride home from work. I was missing the sunshine and began ever so softly singing an old favorite song of John Denver's- back in the 70's. "Sunshine on my Shoulders Makes Me Happy." I had the babies in the back seat- never thinking they could hear much of it. . . but they did. Granddaugher, Gracie Lu asked softly, "Grandma, what were you singing?" I told her- and much to my surprise, she asked me to sing it again. So I did- only this time somewhat louder- not much- but a bit. When I'd finished, Josiah asked me to sing it again. So I did- only this time even louder still. When I finished, they both asked me to sing it yet again. This time I felt such confidence rise up in me that I sang it with an emotional passion. When it ended, I could not help wonder why they had wanted me to sing this song over and over again. I have always known I had not been given a beautiful voice and cannot stay on key for the life of me; yet these two angels had asked me to croon this song four different times. Then, like a crystal clear revelation, it came to me. They had not heard my scratchy voice- they had not even noticed those notes I could not quite make, nor the verses I kept changing around; they had only heard my heart- and they wanted more of it.

I have always believed that whoever sings out to the Lord- whatever note you are singing in, God hears it as if it were in perfect melodious pitch. I wonder, could it possibly be that children are similar in that they too do not hear the off notes—just our hearts—and so they are lulled to sleep, simply comforted as if our voices were the most beautiful music from heaven itself. I have this inner feeling that we underestimate the many spiritual giftings of our children. I mean, if babies can see angels, isn't it possible they can hear our hearts as well?

Just like our lifesong, sometimes we think those small unseen love gestures (like buttering toast for your child or holding a door open for a stranger) are insignificant "off notes" in our life, not amounting to much compared to the famous opera-singing stars of the world. Do not be fooled, for in actuality, YOUR song climbs the highest notes of heaven—you just aren't hearing it like He is. Remember, there are no off-notes in heaven, just people on Earth who THINK they are unimportant in His choir.

we all have our song—so sing! Sing out with everything you have within you. No one can sing it like you can. Never ever allow the world to quiet you!

I will never forget that morning when my two little sweeties asked Grandma something I did not think anyone ever wanted-it was truly a magical moment in time; and I wholeheartedly embraced it. So, for those of you not blessed with a voice like an angel, the next time you sing to your children, remember their little ears hear more than you will ever really know- so sing your little heart out and let Jesus take care of the rest.

IF NOT NOW, THEN WHEN?
(July 11, 2009)

———ᗧᗧ———

O ur world is jammed with procrastinators and dreamers. When I hear someone say, "Someday I want to. . . " or "Someday I will go here or there and do this or that, " I actually get sad and weary inside. I guess because I know most of what is spoken will usually die, like bubbles popping in the wind. So why do we dream and talk big and then move on- as one would do with a parting friend— a hug, a kiss, a wave good-bye and we walk away. But what happened to the long embrace? Why can't we look at our 'some-days' straight in the eyes and turn them around to mean 'Now'? I like the way my sister took a directive from the Lord and ran with it to be a nurse. She is focused and will become one soon; or when my husband, Greg, and I sat down and actually wrote out the years and places we want to visit in the future. This also gives one accountability—the date is set—and so is the place. So many plans have been spoken by people only to have died en route to never-never land. I say if you have enough of a desire to speak it, then maintain your dream with at least one action to keep that dream afloat. If more of us accomplished our dreams, perhaps the phrases: 'pie in the sky,' 'pipe dreaming' and 'in the sweet by and by' would eventually become extinct.

IT'S NOT EASY BEING GREEN
(July 11, 2009)
(HOW TO SURVIVE IN THE WORLD—
ALWAYS FEELING LIKE A SQUARE PEG
IN A ROUND HOLE)

E verywhere I go (and it seems to be getting more intense), I feel a struggle. Exceptions would be in my home and with family and very close friends. With them, I almost feel celebrated for possessing the misfit parts; and a sense of uniqueness washes over me and a most satisfied and contented peace blankets my spirit.

But when I step outside of the 'bubble,' I am starkly reminded of the sharp edges of that square that I am striving to squeeze into. I remember the prophecy over me when this prophetic woman pointed me out in a crowd, lovingly shook her head, and said, 'You, my dear, are a square peg trying your hardest to fit into a round hole!' Of course I started crying because she was right on! Sometimes it is merely a story one is sharing that I did not quite follow (nothing too serious and actually quite able to live with.) Then there are those times I struggle with following driving directions, or even the correct entrance and exit doors. There's also the age old fear of people laughing at me for my actions of stupidity. But there is a bright side to all this. I have Learned to laugh at myself—a round peg in a square hole; perhaps I should try not to resist this poor fit but instead lay the peg down beside the hole and be glad it doesn't fit. I need to celebrate the fact that I am different. These are the moments when words like 'unique,' 'one of a kind,' and 'a broken mold' are birthed. I have been hand crafted by a God who loves me dearly and wants me to rejoice in my differences. Yes, indeed, a round peg in a square hole. You know, as I think more about that, I kind of like the fit after all. It defines me-and my fiber, woven by my Lord Jesus. That is fine with me.

They were strangers and pilgrims on the earth. (Heb. 11:13 NKJV).

DR. CHRISTMAS TREE
(Dec. 2009)

—⁂—

I t started out innocently enough. I had purchased it for $9.00 from my pre-school. We do an annual fund raiser, selling spruce tips, wreaths, and now small trees. I liked the idea of the yard tree and a friend had suggested I put lights on it and place it on our veranda. But I had decided to save money and display it in our great room. When I'd finished stringing the lights, I stood back, hoping the lights would dress it up a bit. It still reminded me of an elderly woman trying her hardest to "dress up" her age with fancy jewelry. So there it stood, ever so feebly in the room. It was truly the ugliest tree I had ever seen—skinny finger-like growths protruding from its stringy branches. Because there really was no back to the tree, I had to keep it tucked against the wall, which made it look even more unattractive.

When I'd picked Faith up from school, she took one look at it and declared, "Mom, this tree is pathetic!"

We both laughed. It was medicine to my shriveled soul. I had not laughed for so long. Throughout the evening, I would just Look at the tree and begin laughing. When my husband returned home, he shook his head and laughed as well.

It was then that I realized the essence of this life lesson. The tree does not mind being laughed at, for it has purpose; and though it is thinning and misshapen, it was chosen to bring joy and laughter to all who enter our home. Some are called to be kings and rule nations. Still, some are called to more lowly positions. In God's eyes, there is no calling more important than another, just be the best at whatever that calling may be. . . like my Dr. Christmas tree, called to give the gift of laughter and giggles and lift spirits.

"A cheerful disposition is good for your health; gloom and doom leave you bone-tired." (Prov. 17:22 The Message Bible)

THOSE GOD-APPOINTMENTS
(Oct. 13, 2009)

—◦◦◦—

I have learned it is seldom the Sunday best-dressed days that God uses me. Instead it is the "not prepared, flip flops" kind of days that those unexpected God moments show up. Allow me to explain:

It was one of those Plain Jane kind of days. Grace, my grand daughter, wanted me to watch her in gymnastics. As I watched, a friendly mom near me struck up a conversation. Before long, I was sharing some life thoughts of my faith. I found myself recommending the awesome devotional, "Jesus Calling" to her. Finally, it was time to go. As I walked away, I felt so strongly that this had been an appointed time. Isn't it awesome to be used by God?

THE CREAKING OF A RUSTY GATE
(Dec. 2009)

—◈—

It had been a fabulous church service–complete with powerful worshipful music and singing-raising arms in praise to my King of Kings. The message had been inspiring as well. Fellowship afterward had also been sweet. But within a mere two hours after all this spiritual ecstasy, we return home and the phone rings. I am disappointed that I had answered it. As I listen to a speech on money needed for the Special Olympics, I robotically and unemotionally interrupt, 'No, I am going to pass this year- good by.' Immediately upon hanging up on him, I verbally expressed my disgust. 'So now we know who that mystery number is that keeps calling us.' Moments later I felt convicted. What just happened? Was the same voice that stood praising God just hours before now interrupting this salesman collecting for a good cause and slamming the receiver down in his ear? Would I have behaved the same way if the man on the other end of my phone had been from my church? Since when did it start being okay to treat strangers at our door and phone solicitors rudely? For some odd and twisted reason, we think that we Christians need to stand up for ourselves and be protected from these "perpetrators" and "scoundrels". What right do they have to take up our time and energy? So we remain in that mindset. It all fits and makes sense until I read here in 1 Corinthians 13:1 "If I speak with human eloquence and angelic ecstasy." For me, that would be if I really got into the worship at church—singing, clapping, raising my voice and arms in praise—but did not speak respectfully and lovingly to strangers. I am the "creaking of a rusty gate." I don't want to be the creaking of a rusty gate to Your ears, Lord. I don't want to sound pious to the listening ears of people I know, yet rude to strangers. They are ALL Your children and You see and hear ALL. Amen!

(1 Cor. 13:1- The Message Bible)

"If I speak with human eloquence and angelic ecstasy but don't love, I'm nothing but the creaking of a rusty gate."

THE CHRISTMAS MIRACLE
(Dec. 13, 2009)

—⁓—

"Test me in this and see if I don't open up heaven itself to you and pour out blessings beyond your wildest dreams." Malachi 3:10b The Message Bible

I t was Sunday, Dec 13th. We had just left our church, where we had dropped off a large supply of bakery that our local grocery store had donated. The supply was generous and I had so wanted to give it to a needy family. We decided to simply drive down to the inner city and pray for the Lord to show us where to go and who to give it to. I recall saying, "Just keep driving and the Lord will guide us to the place or person." I began praying silently, calling on the Lord to help us. Then we turned down a street and discovered it was a dead end. As we were turning around, I noticed a building on our right called, Open Arms. I'd recalled someone at church mentioning it to me. We pulled in.

Many people were there, preparing meals for the terminally ill, those with HIV Aids, Cancer, etc. They were very appreciative of our donation. As we got back into the car, I was amazed at how mighty and personal our God is. He had once again come through. He had actually guided our car to this place- a place God had led us to.

THE WAY OF LOVE—
THE MESSAGE BIBLE
(1 Cor. 13)

—⁓—

I f I speak with human eloquence and angelic ecstasy, but don't love, I'm nothing but the creaking of a rusty gate. If I speak God's Word with power, revealing all His mysteries and making everything plain as day, and if I have faith that says to a mountain, "Jump and it jumps, but I don't love, I'm nothing. If I give everything I own to the poor and even go to the stake to be burned as a martyr, but I don't love, I've gotten nowhere. So, no matter what I say, what I believe, and what I do, I'm bankrupt without love.

Love never gives up. Love cares more for others than for self. Love doesn't want what it doesn't have. Love doesn't strut, doesn't have a swelled head, doesn't force itself on others, isn't always "me first," doesn't fly off the handle, doesn't keep score of sins of others, doesn't revel when others grovel. Love takes pleasure in the flowering of truth, puts up with anything, trusts God always, always looks for the best, never looks back, but keeps going to the end. Love never dies. Inspired speech will be over some day; praying in tongues will end; understanding will reach its limit. We know only a portion of the truth, and what we say about God is always incomplete. But when the complete arrives, our incompletes will be cancelled. When I was an infant at my mother's breast, I gurgled and cooed like any infant. When I grew up, I left those infant ways for good. We don't yet see things clearly. We're squinting in a fog, picking through a mist. But it won't be long before the weather clears and the sun shines bright! We'll see it all then- see it all as clearly as God sees us, knowing Him directly just as He knows us!

But for right now, until that completeness, we have 3 things to do to lead us toward that consummation: Trust steadily in God, hope unswervingly, love extravagantly. The best of the three is love.

THE WATER CARRIER
(Feb 26, 2010)

—⁓—

Dear Lord Jesus- continue to give me the comfort, peace and joy in being comfortable with who I am- all my weirdness, slowness, dramatic emotional actions, and annoying flaws—to know and believe You when You so lovingly whisper, "My grace is sufficient." Lord Jesus, I am privileged to be your helper, your ambassador. Thank you for the analogy of the thirsty. I can pick up the water at the store and give it to the thirsty- though I am not the living water, You are that- but I help carry it to the thirsty- I don't need a fancy crystal pitcher to carry my water—all You ask is a willing heart and time given to You- I can carry my water in the palms of my hands if need be- because I may not always be prepared with a glass or wooden vessel- just that my heart is willing and my hands will carry just the right amount of water to a thirsty soul. Just give to me the privilege of being your water carrier.

Side note: I think it's really important to personally invite Jesus to events. He loves the invitation. It's kind of like having someone be at Your home via telephone or choosing to have Him there IN PERSON—He loves it and He always shows up!

ONCE UPON A TIME

(Feb. 11, 2010)

—∂∂∂—

Once upon a time, there lived a mom- she had 5 children and was blessed with 4 more through her children's mates. They all lived in sweet homes with pretty yards. When they all got together, there was much laughter and love. But sometimes life is sad; and the tears fall. The prayers then go out and the tears are wiped away because of the power of those prayers. When one is hurting, each one would come to her aid in each one's own individual way. It was good and the mom was ever so warmed and mightily blessed by the compassion exhibited. I am that mom; and I just want to thank each and every one of you for blessing me with your caring ways. I am overwhelmed by the compassion I see in my family. As I told my granddaughters, Rachel, and Gracie Lu, (they had come bounding over on Sunday morning with a handful of cards and gifts for their Auntie Faith) 'embrace your gifting of compassion girls-for it is rare in our fast-paced, over-worked, highly distracting world. I just wanted all of you to know that the words and cards mean so much more to us than these words can accurately convey. I tell you, it makes a mother proud, it makes a mother proud. All my love, Mom.'

GRILLED CHEESE
AND FROZEN PEAS
(Feb 2,2010)

———∞∞∞———

I love Best Friends. I love watching them interact together—
each one bouncing back the ball to each other in rhythmic
motion- their spirits flowing in total syncopated union.

We were leaving the pre-school (my grandson and I). He had
played with his best friend, Bentley, effortlessly throughout the
morning, ending with a creative lunch bunch time. I listened to
them as they chattered on about ideas of where this truck should
be and who says what in their little pretend world. Now we were
all headed for our cars- his mommy, my grandson and myself. As
we approached our cars, I heard my grandson's best friend yell,
"I can't wait to eat grilled cheese and frozen peas.!" As we drove
away, I asked Josiah about what Bentley had meant by that. He
replied, "Oh, that's our favorite food."

I love best friends. I have had quite a few myself. My first one was when I was barely 2 years old. She was my cousin and we were completely glued at the hip. Then I started school. I remember Ella. We used to stand on the teeter totter as it went up and down on the playground of our little one room school house. Then there were grade school short- lifer friends—with painful memories of some still etched in my heart. Then there was Cheri. It was 7th grade and we became heart and soul bosom buddies. We did sleep-overs, bike rides, walks and talks. Cheri moved after 8th grade. We saw each other afterwards sparingly and then she walked out of my life. The friendship had become shriveled, and like an unwatered plant, it eventually died. I sometimes think of her and miss her. Then, in high school, I met Hally. We enjoyed four fun years together and have remained friends to this day. In college, a dear friend, Kris, (who I had known since the 4th grade) became my constant buddy, along with a fun-loving girl named La. The three of us clicked, but life has ways of separating boats—and once again, my friends drifted away from me. I became lonely and wanted a best friend in my grown up season. So I prayed to the One who could provide the perfect friend for me. It was very soon after that when I met a lovely woman at the church I was attending. She was soft, caring, pretty, and loved Jesus with all her heart and soul. It was not very long until we knew we had found our own kindred spirits. That was 27 years ago. Sally and I are still together. We have been through massive rocky valleys, where we could barely see any daylight. We've celebrated new life through a birth and one from adoption. We have been there at our children's marriages, renewing of vows, life threatening poor health, struggles in our personal lives, saying goodbye to parents, houses, and job losses by husbands. There isn't very much we have not walked through hand in hand together. We have taken our turns in holding each other up when one of us could not stand on her own. We call this our "journey" and we walk it together.

The other day I had mentioned to her, "I sometimes have glimpses of the two of us, walking together in heaven and talking about the "journey" and how we made it through.

Yes, I love the sound of "Best Friend". I even host a Best Friends Retreat each year- to celebrate this very thing. Though our favorite foods may not be "grilled cheese and frozen peas," I think just sitting together at her kitchen table, sipping herbal tea and tiny cookies or banana bread comes pretty darn close.

GRANDMA REMEMBERS

QUOTES FROM MY GRANDCHILDREN

—ово—

Josiah (Feb 3, 2010)

"**G**uess what, if God made me like others, then there would be no one like me."

(Spoken to Grandma as I was driving him to pre-school with me)

"The other tomorrow" (4 year old Rachel's way of saying, "the day after tomorrow".

IN MEMORIUM-
OUR MILKY WAY
(Feb 5, 2010)

—ɷɷ—

It is now 24 hours since we lost our beautiful silky golden and white hamster named Milky Way. I remember the day we got her. Daughter Faith was 12 years old and we were looking at all these various hamsters. Then Faith spotted her- smooth and silky. She was placed in a box and brought home. We put her in a cage and were told to allow her to acclimate for approximately 24 hours. We did, sort of- but could not wait that long. Soon after, she managed to escape in Faith's bathroom through a tiny crack in the vanity base. We panicked and prayed. My son Josh came dashing over and tried to pry apart the vanity baseboard. Then, miraculously, she crept out. Josh grabbed her and it was good-except she had developed a respiratory infection; so the vet checked her, prescribed medicine and she got better. However, because of the medicine, she lost her teeth. So there we were, crushing up her food. But we did not know that hamster teeth grow back and we loved her so. We had fun feeding her broccoli and apples. If she were snuggled in her upstairs wheel bed, all I would have to do is talk to her and she would plow herself down- she knew our voices. We knew 2 years was her given life span; and when Oct., 2009 came and went, I realized we were on borrowed time. Almost every day I would pray over her with a: "God bless you, God bless you."

Then, quite unexpectedly, on Thursday, Feb 4, I returned home from work to find Faith crying- saying our little Milky Way was very sick. She was convulsing and throwing up green. Faith had been holding her for one hour. I diagnosed it as a stroke. We brought her to the veterinary clinic because we did not want her suffering. They said she was struggling to breathe. They let us privately say our good-byes. Faith held her. I talked to her; she became quite energized and tried so hard to be strong. She seemed to say, "I love you too- thank you for giving to me a good life- I will be fine." We then released her. After the euthanasia was complete, they put her in a box, along with her little paw prints, and gave her back to us. We then cried and cried and cried. Milky Way, you won a place in our hearts and we will love you always.

THE PRINCESS DRESS
(PART 1)

—⚬⚬⚬—

I remember feeling like a real princess- especially with my daddy. I was an only child for 7 whole years. . . 'daddy's girl'. We went everywhere together- to a baseball game, to the store and frequently the 100-mile road trip to Chicago, where my Pappo and Grandma lived. They too made me feel very special and beautiful. Being their only granddaughter, I was given much attention and coddling.

Sometimes my daddy would lift me up over his head and put me on his shoulders; or he would lie on his back and bring his legs up and suspend me on my tummy and my hands would hold onto his hands. I felt like I was flying. Then there were the times he would curl my hair. (daddy would not allow my mom to cut it). When my hair dried and he'd remove the curlers, my hair would literally bounce with curls- I had my daddy's curly hair genes too! I remember when he would stand behind me and tell me to fall back into his ever waiting arms. It was hard to do; but I trusted him to catch me, which he unfailingly always did. Then there are the times he would tickle my feet until I could barely breathe. To this day, I know he probably tickled all the tickles out of me.

Then I started school; and I learned quite quickly just what the word 'bullying' looked and felt like. I wondered, 'How could anyone tease and call bad painful names to my daddy's princess? Don't they know I'm daddy's girl?'

My princess dress was beginning to feel scratchy, but I kept it on because, well, that's just what princesses do.

But somewhere between the tears of homesickness, not fitting in and struggling with learning, the dress slipped quietly off my shoulders. I hardly even noticed; for I had adapted to wearing this different dress now- it had words splashed all over it: stupid, inadequate, unpopular, ugly, homesick, poor, crooked teeth, big nose, bad breath, old house, foreign looking daddy, ugly name,— the list could go on and on. I had soon adjusted to the fit and lived with this different dress most of the time now. I say 'most of the time' because there were those occasions when the dress would stay on, but the words would slip off- like when I was with my friends, having a party, or laughing. But when I would return to school, they would magically reappear. Often I would envy those girls parading around in their princess gowns- wishing so much to have mine back.

Then one day it happened. I boldly walked into my closet, dusted off my gown and slipped it on. It was a perfect fit- I had almost forgotten what it felt like to walk around feeling pretty, bright, happy and giggly. The world looked different- from the lonely black and white to neon sparkle; and life was good.

I am still wearing that dress. True, it's not quite as billowy, crisp and new—and it has yellowed a bit with age. Like wearing one's original wedding gown decades later, it doesn't hang quite the same, nor does the body fill it up in quite the same way. There are some holes, a few rips here and there and perhaps some may even say it has a bit of a tattered face to it. But it is mine, and wears the reality of my life—in all of its ashes, in all of its beauty. The beauty of my gown is not only seen by what the human eye can see, it is also felt by what the heart remembers.

Me and my princess dress- if you look ever so closely- you can still see the shimmer, the glisten, the sparkle . You just have to look a bit closer.

FOR ALL THE PRINCESS DRESSES
THAT HANG IN THE CLOSETS
PART #2
(August 2, 2010)

I was at Cub foods today and saw a balloon with the caption: "A new little Prince."- Under that it read: "A new little Princess." It would be a balloon to be presented to the parents of a newborn. As I stood looking at them, I could not prevent my mind from traveling back to a few days ago. I had been invited to my granddaughter Gracie Lou's Princess Dance Recital. When I arrived, I saw all the little girls dressed in their favorite princess attire-twirling, whirling, circling and doing a dance that, princesses are created to do. It was darling. When my daughter and I returned to the car, we began talking about when girls (and boys) begin to have their princess and prince dreams shattered—and when the world begins to tell them that they are not what they thought they were. We both shared our stories- and my younger daughter, later, shared hers as well. I began thinking of my sons; I could probably guess when their tuxedos had been taken away.

I guess because of this life in its fallen state, one cannot expect to be able to hold unto this truth for long. I would like to think that for everyone who has had their prince and princess mirrors shattered, there is also a time when it becomes restored—perhaps even given a new mirror—and the image that one sees shines even brighter still. Even when those voices return, attempting to smash the image, it remains intact because of a firmer and stronger truth woven through. If we could only cement the truth of truths (Jesus) into our hearts. You see us as Your sons and daughters. Since You are King Jesus, we are indeed your princesses and princes. The world may continue to attempt to erode this truth, but we need to stand firm in confidence, boldness, and courage. If only we could all walk into our closets, dust off our gowns and tuxedos, and wear them with a renewed and inner assurance. Dance ever so gracefully; see how lovely your dresses sway with the music of your life path—it was made for you and no one else can wear it as beautifully as you.

THE WORLD WAKES
(Sunday, May 16, 2010)

———⌘———

Oh Lord the world is absolutely bursting with life- alive in your glory! I wake early (before 6:00) to the melodious sounds of Your birds- Robins, Purple Finch, Yellow Finch- Yesterday I did what I so love to do best- plant my flowers. I could not wait to get out there. As I planted these beauties on my veranda, I listened to Your symphony—the world comes alive and Your birds proclaim its awakening.

I wonder, do people really hear Your choir? As I write this, I am being beautifully serenaded by these winged creatures. Last evening two morning doves sang their love songs to each other. Have you ever wondered how quiet and lonely spring would be without the sounds of these sweet ones? Have we grown so accustomed to them that we have reduced the level of their presence to a mere 'white noise'?—like a restaurant bursting with people's chatter? Do we go about our days totally oblivious to their melodies? Oh Lord, if I can awaken to their songs, then I have partaken in a preview of what awaits me in glory. Why does everything have to come with a price? I mean—here it is spring—and I am so tuned to its every movement- the first buds on our decorative crab apple trees- fresh spikes poking from my flower bed- the croons from our feathered friends . But here's the question: Do we have to go through a winter to really and truly appreciate a spring—does everything come with a price?

INSPIRATIONS BY FAITH BROWN
(MY BEAUTIFUL DAUGHTER)
(June 26th 11:09 PM)

—◦ᴥ◦—

LIGHTENING is not afraid to show itself.

THUNDER is not afraid to be heard.

RAIN is not afraid to affect things around it.

B ut people, people are afraid to be seen, heard, and cause others to move.

I want to be one of those people who isn't afraid to be seen, heard, or make them move.

DOG POOP AND A GARAGE SALE
(July, 2010)

———✎———

It was the lovely month of July and had the feel of a lazy kyros day. As my grandson, Josiah and I laid on a blanket at a nearby park playing cards, I could not help thinking how blessed I was. Suddenly, my daughter Faith came walking over, saying she had injured her arm. It looked puffy and she was in obvious pain. The morning ended abruptly. But as we packed up to leave, I noticed my oldest granddaughter, Rachel, crying. I found out she was feeling sad because she felt it was her fault. "Why?" I asked. "Because we were running, and she said to stop and I didn't." I quickly told her it was not her fault and teasingly added that it was mine, "Because I'm the one that had suggested we go to the park." She continued to cry and feel sad. Then I thought of a great analogy. "Say Rachel, you know how you love garage sales? (and she really does)-well, what if you walked into one that was actually selling dog poop, would you buy it?" She quickly replied,

"No!" "Well, then why do you buy or believe this lie that Satan is telling you? It's the same as 'buying dog poop?'"

IT'S ALL IN THE LETTING GO - SOMETIMES REPEATEDLY
(Aug 16, 2010)

———◈◈◈———

I remember thinking, "if I could just give this whole problem up to Jesus, I would feel lighter and free of this long burdensome heaviness." Finally, after many years, I had the courage to do just that, feeling free and light. I also saw the results I had been praying for. I began proclaiming His never ending goodness, telling everyone how I had given the worry to Him and he had then answered my prayers. Little did I know that I would be faced with having to give the same problem up to Him again and again. So here I go Lord—the problem is back and so am I, handing it over to You. It's all in the persevering of the letting go.

THE 500 HATS OF GOOD OLD BARTHOLOMEW
(Sept, 2010)

—◈—

I had been talking to my son, Josh, about trusting Jesus and not taking on worries and cares that are meant to be left to Him. I flippantly said, "Sometimes we become like good old Bartholomew Cubbins," to which Josh replied, "How's that? All I remember is that he wore many hats." So I proceeded to read the book. It seems Bartholomew, preparing to bow to the king, removed his hat, but, curiously, another hat magically appeared on his head. This made the king furious and was going to have poor Bartholomew executed, but since he could not keep his head hatless, the executioner could not kill him. Then the hats changed; they became fancier and fancier and the king became very fond of Bartholomew's hats—all 500 of them! Finally, the last hat appeared on Bartholomew's head—solid gold—which the king readily purchased.

I think we all need to stop wearing hat after hat of worries and fears. I know Jesus wants us to wear just one hat—that of trusting Him. All others will weigh us down. Jesus doesn't want us wearing what has not been given to us. As in the case of poor old Bartholomew, let's all hand the hats over to the King!

AT THE RIGHT PLACE
(Monday, Oct. 4, 2010)

—⁓—

I personally define a miracle as something unexplainable that happens in a God-timed manner with events so clock-worked by Him that afterwards you sit back and go, "Wow, what was that all about?"

I had picked Faith up at school and we then drove to Curves. Upon returning home, I noticed I had a message on my phone. After listening to it, I'd discovered I had inadvertently brought home another woman's sport bag. I grabbed it and headed out the door—only to see my dear neighbor friend and her daughter about to begin a walk. They had made it to the end of my driveway. I knew she had been waiting to hear from the Mayo Clinic regarding her cancer check-up. I looked at her and asked, "Did you hear?" She said she had just hung up from talking to them. She said, "I can't talk." She then buried her head on my shoulder. I recall saying to her, "You don't have to talk." I was the first to learn that she had just been told she had been given 6 to 12 months to live. I then proceeded to tell her how glad I was we had Jesus and reminded her about the International Healing Conference coming up this Wednesday through Saturday. When I returned home from dropping off the sport bag, I could not help but feel God had specifically hand-picked me to be the one to comfort her in her first moments of receiving this horrifying news. Thank you, Jesus! I can really see your fingerprints in this one.

NOTHING IS EVER WASTED

(Oct. 25–30 2010)

———✺———

Being suddenly thrust into emotional pain, I had made a choice, with the help of Jesus, to outright trust Him emphatically. I remember hearing His words to me. "I'm in this; believe my promises." I took each day at a time, trusting Him completely. I felt His presence and when I felt myself begin to spiral down, I would call on Him to hold me steady. On Saturday, my trial ended and I felt like I had passed a huge milestone in my life path. "Perhaps I won't need to go around that same mountain again," I'd thought. More blessings were yet to come.

On Sunday, as I sat in church, I felt Jesus was going to be using me to meet a prayer need of someone. So when my Pastor announced for all those on the prayer ministry to come forward, I bolted. Sure enough, as my husband and I stood up front, a precious woman walked up and requested prayer. My life lesson of fully trusting Jesus was still so new in my heart. I confidently shared with her how the #1 gift we can give to Jesus in to fully trust Him. I felt I had the authority to speak about it, like I had 'paid the price.' Now I was to pass this on to someone who needed to hear it too. "So, (I continued), when one travels through the scary black forest, I encourage you to always know that He is in it all- and He is doing a work through it. The hard times are never wasted."

I so believe this; I must believe this. Life is too short for any wasted moments. He will use it all for His glory!

WINDOWS IN TIME

(Nov. 16, 2010)

—⦿—

Everybody has them, those peek-holes of opportunities for us to choose whether we want to grab it or not, like speaking truth, love, and encouragement to a person via a hug, words of life, or the urging to send that thank you. Sometimes it is not really spiritual but none the less, a "window-like" whispering voice (Holy Spirit) that calls us into action. I pray for more courage to recognize these moments.

Windows In Time. They are always there in our lives, if we could only recognize their significance

AS I AWAIT THE PHONE CALL

(Nov. 16, 2010)

—⟪⟫—

On Oct. 12, 2010, I kept my cell phone glued to my body. I was awaiting "the call". That call would tell me my 10th grandbaby had arrived—a new life from the arms of Jesus to our family here on earth. As I watched my preschoolers play so freely outside, that special call did indeed come. It came with an announcement of joy and tears- a feeling of relief- all labor had ceased- baby had arrived safely and was now in the arms of mommy. All is well. The Lord has given!

It is the eve of Nov. 16th and once again I await "the call". This call will be somewhat the same, yet also painfully different. This call will tell me about a life, but the announcement will come packaged in tears. Yes, there will be a feeling of relief that all laboring in death is over and my precious friend had arrived safely home and into the arms of her Daddy. All is well. The Lord has given and the Lord has taken away.

Terry went to her everlasting home to be with her Jesus, the love of her life, on Tuesday at 4:15 PM.

I AM CONVINCED
Nov. 20, 2010

—⟋∿⟍—

As I look back on my life, I realize that I have lived through births, precious loved one's deaths, saying good-bye to loving pets, indescribable joys, betrayals, answered prayers, disappointments, heartaches, heart breaks, a broken heart, depression, loneliness, fears, unsurpassed peace, oceanic love, an emptied heart, overflowing heart, insecure to comfortable, prayers hitting a silent ceiling to personally feeling His presence—His words of peace and comfort prophetically and divinely spoken over me.

In all of life's deepest dark forests to sunrise peaked mountain tops, I have arrived at 3 friends that must walk with you. The first is my faith in a Jesus that keeps His promises when He says He will never ever leave you—2nd- to be able to forgive- now this one is hard; so you must draw from His reservoir that never goes empty. 3rd- to guard your heart. I think it is like this: certain people that hurt and harm need to be forgiven, yet also kept at arm's length. It is quite tricky; for you still need to allow the love of Jesus to shine through you. I guess it is a process that one never really masters but always pushes for.

A TRIBUTE TO MY FRIEND, TERRY
(who went to be with Jesus on Nov.16, at 4:15th PM)

—⟨≈⟩—

In the month of November- on Thanksgiving Day, I met you Terry. You had invited our entire family over for this feast. I could not believe there was someone living in this world that would be so gracious and generous to invite a family she had never met over for Thanksgiving. I loved you immediately. It seemed our spirits connected. I felt valued, treasured and for Some reason young, as in High-School-girl young. Your child-like open-faced faith consumed you and all who came near you.

As time went on, we constructed rich memories of home-made breakfasts at each other's homes, (yours, daughter Jessica's and mine). There were picnics in various parks and a special birthday lunch at Antiquity rose. I remember surprising you with a picture of the Laughing Jesus. You unwrapped it and began lovingly kissing the print. Now you are able to truly see Him face to face, and embrace and kiss your King.

As I close my eyes, I can see you dancing. Your beautiful long hair flowing- and you are pain free.

Someday soon or someday later, I will once more see your sweet face. We two shall embrace, laugh, and walk those golden streets.

But until then, Terry, I will always hold you tightly and dearly in my heart of hearts. I know I will always miss you. I know I will always love you.

Dee

"For My thoughts are not your thoughts, nor are your ways My ways," says the Lord. For as the heavens are higher than the earth, so are My ways higher than your ways; And My thoughts than your thoughts." (Isa. 55:8–9 NKJV).

My Dear Angel Friend, Terry,
who now is home with Jesus.

YOU HAVE BEEN GIVEN TODAY-
NEVER PUT OFF SPEAKING A
WORD OF THANKS, KINDNESS, OR
ENCOURAGEMENT TO SOMEONE
(Feb 28, 2011)

Standing at the hair salon desk, I'd noticed a framed writing of a former employer there. She had been tragically killed in a horrible car accident that involved her and a semi. She had died instantly. As I studied her picture, I realized I had had a conversation with her just weeks before. I remember feeling frustrated that the hair designer I had been waiting for had left for home because she had no clients. I was upset and in a bad mood. Then this lovely young girl had been so understanding and patient with me- apologizing and assuring me she would be there for me tomorrow. When I returned the following day, I thanked her for her kindness and patience with me- that she had given the place "class" and made it look good. She gave me a big smile and thanked me. Now, as I shockingly gaze at her memorial write up, I realize I had no regrets. I had not shirked the nudging to make her day and tell her that her kindness mattered a great deal to me.

MY SWEET LITTLE GRACIE LU

—◈—

Things she said to grandma while riding in the car to and from pre-school (September-May- 2010–2011)

5 Years Old

1. "Grandma, I wish I could live closer to you." To which I said, "But you do live close." Gracie Lu replied, "I want to live next door."
2. "Grandma, will I look the same or different when I get big?"
3. "I can't believe that Meg Rose and I have the same grandma."
4. "My mommy made a good choice in who she married."
5. "Grandma, how can we leave so early and be so late?" (March 23, 2011)
6. "Grandma, how do people make M&M's?" (3–28–11)

7. Grandma: "I've got two little angels in the car with me." Gracie Lu: "Grandma you have a real angel too—one that watches over you."

I have so enjoyed being able to share a piece of Gracie's and Ben's life this past year. We have become close and I trust that it is a bond that time and distance will not take form me. So, thank you for allowing me this privilege. I will forever treasure the year when the three of us shared a common love—Grandma's pre-school.

SOMETIMES GOD'S GIFTS COME IN LITTLE PACKAGES
(Sat. June 5, 2010)

—⟨∿⟩—

Early one Monday morning, my granddaughter, Rachies, called me on the phone (about 7:30 AM) saying she wanted to take me to Target and buy me something special. We'd agreed on noon, but she soon changed it to 9:00 AM. It was a lovely day. We walked to Target together. When we arrived, I mentioned I had to get some stuff first. Rachies thought she should buy my stuff, but I convinced her otherwise. Then we went over to the $1.00 area. She slipped $1.25 into my pocket, but I returned it to her. I picked out a lovely yellow veggie tray. She said she wanted to treat me to something at the snack bar too. I had a yogurt parfait. She had a cherry and lime icee. Then we looked at the toy section. She wanted a pet shop toy. She didn't have enough money; I surprised her and bought it for her. Then we walked to the library and got some "bird books." We then walked home. What a treasure of a day. Thank you Jesus. I felt loved.

LET'S LOVE ON
THE MCQUOIDS DAY
(Feb. 6, 2011)

—⟨∿⟩—

Tami, Mattrick, Rachies, Josiah, Gracie Lu and Ben—This is your day to feel loved on and appreciated. A couple weeks ago, I felt this urge to surprise you by having everyone over just to celebrate all of you. The plans were completed in a matter of minutes- as most everyone responded so readily.

Please allow me a few minutes as I express the words my heart has been suppressing for some time now. Perhaps it won't be easy, perhaps there will be tears; but sometimes through Tears, we feel released, revived, and refreshed, so here it goes.

I recall it well- some friends were desperately trying to get out from under the payments of their house. We were given the opportunity to check it out—we looked but declined. Shortly afterward, you surprised us with the news that you were buying it. I could not be happier. We called it the 'party house'—and rightly so- as you both had earned the reputation as being a family who absolutely loved to entertain. All the house needed next were memories—and they began to burst forth almost immediately. There were parties to celebrate birthdays, (remember our Chris dressed as a clown?) parties to celebrate upcoming weddings, parties to celebrate upcoming babies, not to mention surprise parties (one for Matt- one for Tami)- we cannot forget The New Year's Eve party- our first white elephant event- and all the 4th of July extravaganzas- Chris's fire works and bubble maker- and the children completely covered in bubbles as they went sliding down the homemade slide Matt had constructed. There was the Bible Study, Bible (Captivating) that you and I lead together. I can recall one scary evening getting a phone call that Rachies was very sick. I ran over to find the two of you in the bathroom- steaming the poor little thing. She had Whooping cough; we prayed together and trusted our Lord to heal her, which He did do. I recall Rachies learning to ride a two-wheeler and how proud she looked as she rode down her grassy slope in the backyard. In the backyard: snowmen and swing sets, a flower patch I'd planted from the flowers the Captivating gals surprised you with, and sledding down the hill at a winter's birthday party for Rachies. In the front yard: Lemonade stands, garage sales, talking on the front porch, and just seeing the children outside on the play yard as I'd drive by your house. As I would pass by,

I'd always thank the Lord for this ultimate gift and promise I would never ever take it for granted.

But life has a way of never moving in a straight line for long. Sooner or later, there will be curves—some sharp, some not so much. Sometimes the road is smooth as an icy slope, but never for long. Potholes and steep embankments have a way Of appearing. I know because we live in this world and so we (as you put it, Tami) ride out the waves which brings me to just where we are today.

Today I want to tell you how much I love you. I want to unswervingly tell you why and try my best to plant my words deeply into your hearts.

Mattrick: Thank you for your emergency visits to our home. As I think back, I don't know what I would have done without your sacrificial house calls. Thank you for even agreeing to live close to me. I realize many sons in law would never even consider it. Because of this, you have given to me a treasure chest of memories. Thank you for showing to me what integrity, realness, truthfulness, trusting, waiting, loving, daddy, provider, husband, awesome sense of humor, and Jesus lover looks like!

Tami: You are my Tami Dawn. You own a good share of my heart. I know I love you way too much and my heart has burst a thousand times with pride as I'd introduce you to this person and that one. You live what you preach and never pretend to know it all. Your favorite word is "season" and it is the perfect description for the many shifts, episodes, interludes, and phases we all walk through in our lifetimes. You teach the world what outrageous and extravagant giving looks like. You show how to be a mommy without losing it and yelling, but instead speaking with kindness, love, and patience. You show me how to be true to oneself even when it hurts, how to listen to Jesus and be obedient to His soft voice, and how to pray over people with everything you have. Thank you for your laughter; it has been as medicine to me.

Rachies, Josiah, Gracie-Lu and Ben: you are and will always be Grandma's little angels; and although I will not see those little bikes come riding down grandma's sidewalk, I know we will have a whole new world of memories yet to be shaped. So let's all take Jesus' hand and see what's just around the corner, for He's always full of surprises.

Love, Mom, Dee, and Grandma

HE WHO PLANTS THE SEED

I remember the feeling, that constant ache and emptiness inside. Like a child in an amusement park, I longed for just "one more ride".

I had joined the ranks of the many women longing to have another child. I had been blessed with four beautiful children. Yet, this emptiness prevailed. It got to a point that I would fall apart when I would see any baby while out shopping. Something had to be done.

I remember my best friend praying that if this ache inside of me were not from God, that He would remove this intense longing. It just grew more intense.

In the middle of all the tears, I had been given a pamphlet on an adoption agency. I simply tucked it away. We soon found a doctor who was willing to perform the needed surgery, a tubal reversal, on my aging body. Still, one year later, we found our-selves in the same place. I continued my relentless prayers.

It was then that I recalled the adoption pamphlet I had previously tucked away. Could God be redirecting our journey? As we entered the agency, my husband and I both felt we were now on course where Jesus wanted us to be.

We had much work in preparation for her arrival. There were home studies to be completed, paperwork that would not quit, interviews that squeezed every ounce of who we are. But it was all so worth it. Approximately 9 months later, on my mother's birthday, the phone rang to proclaim the long awaited news: they have a baby girl for us- born on my birthday!

Our beautiful Guatemalan daughter is now 14 years old. From the first moment they placed that 8 ½ month old angel in our arms, she has continued to be our constant reminder of God's tender, never-ending faithfulness.

Some days, when I feel alone and unheard, all I have to do is look at my beauty queen. Now it all makes sense. It WAS God who placed that desire in my heart; and it would be Him to fill it.

God is faithful. He really does 'have our backs,' and wants to live in every corner of our lives; He is indeed a God of completeness.

Oh, by the way, if you are wondering what we named her: Faith! Surprised?

"Trust God from the bottom of your heart; don't try to figure out everything on your own. Listen for God's voice in everything you do, everywhere you go; He's the one who will keep you on track."

Proverbs 3:5–6 The Message Bible.

A DAY AT THE BEACH
April 8, 2010

—⁓⁓—

She spoke in wisdom and clear insight. So I sat, soaked and listened. I knew You were speaking to me through her- something about the timing- something about her words. They seemed to penetrate into a place I was finally understanding. I believe it was a God-appointed, God ordained time. I feel different- less weighted down; and all because one beautiful woman, who just happens to be my daughter, was courageous and bold enough to tell me 'head on' words that I needed to hear. Her words were to give me new life- and indeed they have. It is the springtime of the year; and it is the springtime of me as well. I look around and see God's re-creating in my garden, on the trees, along the roadside and within my heart. The fresh fragrance known as spring, the freedom of finally understanding— known as rebirth— what could be more freeing!

THE NAME GAME
MY BABIES

—⁓—

CHRISTOPHER: Awesome young man- was Christ-like from birth- lives for Jesus each and every day- gentle and soft spirit. When he was 4 years old, he was performing at our church Christmas program, crying through each and every word of the song, 'Jesus Loves Me.' Suddenly, the music director put the microphone right up to his little mouth; and so he cry-sang the entire song. He was so brave.

TAMI: vivacious, passionate for life, zealous in her walk with the Lord. When Tami was 3 or 4 years old, she would walk up to me and hug my legs as I would wash dishes. This went on for some time; and one day I asked her why she came and hugged me. She lovingly replied, "Because Jesus told me to."

JESSICA: This beautiful daughter loves Jesus with a depth few of us know. When Jessica was a little girl, she would always say that she feels homesick for heaven. Jess has a very intimate relationship with her Savior. One day she announced she felt the family was not complete. I did not understand this feeling she had. But quite a few years later, we did adopt a baby girl from Guatemala—which then completed her picture.

JOSHUA: Josh has been given the gift of a joyous spirit- you cannot remain sad if you are in his presence. He has been the reason why the muscles in my stomach have ached, because of unquenchable laughter. When he turned 21, we surprised him with the Sunday newspaper that came out when he was born. He quickly paged through it to get to the want ad section, looked up cars for sale and actually called the party that had been selling the car some 21 years ago!

FAITH: Faith is our long and hard prayed-for miracle baby from Guatemala. We feel very strongly that she has been hand picked by Jesus for us. Faith has been given a multitude of prophetic gifts. When she was placed in our arms for the first time some 12 ½ years ago, she never cried, but instead had calming peace about her, as if she knew she would be ours and we would love her so.

Thank you Jesus for my babies- they are the very essence of who, what and where I am today.

"Don't you see that children are God's best gift? The fruit of the womb His generous legacy? Like a warrior's fistful of arrows are the children of a vigorous youth. Oh, how blessed are you parents, with your quivers full of children! Your enemies don't stand a chance against you; you'll sweep them right off your doorstep." Psalm 127:3–5 The Message Bible

A LETTER TO MY FIRST BORN SON, ON THE BIRTH OF HIS FIRST BORN SON

Saturday, July 23, 2011

—◦◦◦—

My dear Precious son- I have been reliving the moments: "Grandma, meet your new grandson, Liam Christopher." As you gently placed him in my ever-waiting arms, I saw such pride and grace in your loving face that I could barely contain my emotions. But please allow me to retrace my "life steps" for a few moments.

If ever there were a baby waited and prayed for, it was you, my dear son. With each passing month, I gathered more momentum for the time I would actually be able to see you face to face. Then you arrived, in your own time, and I had to wait even more to gaze into your face, wrap my arms around you, and caress you. But when that time came for me, the world stopped because it was like I was changed forever. I knew I would never be what I was when I'd entered that hospital. I had become a mother of an angel son who changed my heart, mind, and soul.

You grew in softness, wisdom, and grace. I discovered I had been given a very rare and special son. In this world of so many "same's" and "ditto's" and "copy cats," Jesus had chosen me to raise an *original*. I felt called apart from the rest of the whirlwind called life.

As you grew, I realized you carried with you large portions of Jesus. Your wisdom would not have come from any other source—many times I stood amazed at your insight and how you would piece puzzles together so life would, "make sense". Confirmation after confirmation would pop up—reminding me of my original revelation: The Lord had chosen me to raise, mold, and love a rare and special son.

Time and the steps of life marched in rhythmic motion and your longing for that special someone became increasingly evident. We both began a passionate prayer walk—trusting and knowing the Lord who had given you to me, would also, in His time, bring to you the one He had fashioned from the start for you. The key here was, "In His Time". That was the hard part. We waited and prayed and trusted and believed.

I remember the phone call. It went something like this: "Mom, there's someone I want to bring home. We've talked a long time and she fits all the areas that I feel are important to me." The rest of the story is quite funny; that very weekend, right during family prayer, I began thanking the Lord for honoring our years of prayers for that special one, and how she is here. Everyone thought I was being quite presumptuous, but I didn't care—I knew. I just knew! (Kind of like when I knew that your son, Liam, would be a boy.)

So, here we are today. As I stare and stare and stare at this new life, I cannot help but revisit the past pages of my own with you.

Son, I could not be happier for you. You mean everything to me and when I see you so happy, my heart leaps with joy and gratitude. So, on this lovely day in July, I just want you to know that life could never ever be more fulfilling for me than to see, touch, hold, and kiss the first born son of my first born son. I love you, my Brownerella, you hold my heart in your hands.

ADVICE GIVEN TO A FRIEND SOON TO HAVE HER BABY

(March 27, 2011)

———∽∾∿∽———

My Dear Sweet Heidi-

I always find it interesting, when I am asked to give advice for the new bride to be, and in your case a new mom to be. I think people try to make things more complicated than it needs to be. So please accept my rather humble and simplistic advice.

In all of this advice, try your hardest not to strive to be like this person or like that 'super mom'—for it will totally steal your joy and peace in whom God has designed your own individual style to be. Just let that shine.

Speaking of 'shine'—Remember, Heidi—all the teaching and preaching and verbal directing that parents seem so urgent to enforce, does not amount to a hill of beans if they themselves are not living and breathing a Christ-centered lifestyle. Children are watching and listening, in moments when we are not aware that they are. That is what they will learn from—those 'silent teachable moments'—those times when we don't think they are noticing (but they are, and they are taking notes.) Children of Today want the AUTHENTIC, the 'real deal'; and we need to show them that we live and breathe what we say and teach.

To sum all of this up, just be YOU! Oh my goodness, just let that HEIDI SHINE, SHINE, SHINE, AND THIS BABY WILL GROW IN SUCH GRACE, BEAUTY, LOVE AND GENTLENESS that he will carry the name of Jesus by his very presence.

Soon you will hold new life, straight from the very hands of our Jesus—pray yourself silly and watch how He will always give you just the needed grace for each new day. Remember Heidi- His mercies are new each and every morning.

MY DEAR PRECIOUS DAUGHTER, MY TAMI DAWN

Aug. 2, 2011

—~~~—

I t is early Tuesday morning. Faith is sleeping and dad is doing his elliptical. I have come to the place that I have been ever so fearful for, that of saying goodbye to you. Knowing myself, I find solace in writing a closure to this whole waiting period from whence I knew you were leaving. Thank you for opening your heart to me and sharing your deepest innermost dreams. They have played a huge part in my accepting this change in our lives. Now I want to look back on memories too poignant to close the book on just yet. . . not yet.

Remember sitting out on your drive-way with dear family and friends and doing garage sales—the laughter, the lunches, the work, the lemonade stands with cookies? Remember my birthday present—running shoes and an opportunity to "run with you"? I can still see you (if I happened to look out my window at just the right time), running past our house-with a smooth and experienced glide, ponytail bobbing, earphones in place; I remember sharing our very own 'Captivating' Bible Study, and planting the flowers they'd given you out in the back yard. Remember the spur of the moment bon fire in your fire pit? Driving to the Science Museum with the kids, and going to garage sales. I remember one of your children did not have shoes, so I carried them. Remember the trolley that one summer, and our little jaunt with it? Family prayer at your home and the notebook that Matt would read of past prayer requests—all the birthday parties, New Year's Eve parties, surprise parties, baby showers, bridal showers, and my emergency run to your house in the wee hours of the morning (Rachies had croup). Babysitting, cinnamon sticks, and sanctioned toys under beds. There were Legos and Lego creations, books you were currently reading and those completed (stacked in a basket in the living room). I recall the smell of breakfast cooking each time I would come to pick up the kids for pre-school with Ben in his high-chair—eggs strewn about. Sometimes you would ask me to listen to this 'really neat song'. I can still see Matt busy in his office, talking to a customer. Then there was your brother Josh, down in the basement at his make-shift desk in the office, the big swimming pool on the deck and the kids playing in the little one with towels hanging on chairs. A table and umbrella inviting fellowship with friends, and sitting around it eating burgers

Matt had grilled on the big grill. There would usually be a few summer flowers in paper cups desperately trying to survive. A big swing set with added features Matt had made—and a bubble party with Chris's bubble-maker (I can still see the kids sliding down their slide, covered in a white blast of bubbles—giggles and smiles abounding.). Remember all those heart to heart talks around your kitchen table, and on your porch? Remember the summer we went to Walmart and you bought red geraniums for Your deck planters? I can still see those gorgeous bright red flowers in your black rod-iron planters hanging from your deck. I can still see Matt cutting the lawn and you out relaxing on your deck. I remember driving by and seeing the children playing happily on their swing set—or sand box or both. Sometimes I would be driving by and the kids would run out to the edge of the grass to just say 'Hi' and I would blow them a kiss. There was bike riding and Rachel coming over to ask Faith if she'd like to go on a bike ride with her. I can see Matt go driving down the road, the truck and trailer in tow. I always loved surprising you guys with homemade desserts now and then—especially your favorite ooey gooey Rhubarb Delight! I can close my eyes and see each room and your love of decorating. Life was good—I was ever so spoiled—and I knew it!

But life never stays the same—because we're not in heaven yet. So each one of us is given places in our lives when TRUST takes on a new meaning. It becomes less trite sounding and more 'life preserving.' This is where I am currently. For it is in this room of trust that I will survive and eventually flourish. It is truly a place where each Christian must walk if they live in this world; (some go deeper into this room than others.)

Tami, my beautiful daughter, if you have actually gotten to this place in my letter, I thank you, for it is long and perhaps, somewhat tedious, like a story that you've heard over and over and over again. But you know that is how I'm made. I need closure—no loose ends—always closure.

So Tami, on this day, I just want you to know that my love for you cannot ever be quenched, no matter distance, no matter time, no matter tears. No matter, no matter, no matter. It will always burn brightly and strong. If, perhaps, God does choose to call you back "home," I will stand at my front door with wide open arms and tears streaming down my face. I will welcome you back in my arms for you will always be my Tami Dawn. Though your dreams may take you far away, you will always be my Tami Dawn, my little girl running to the sandbox, chubby legs a going. I love you!

My Dear Precious Son- Josh Krosh Mosh Rosh (written to my son after I had completed his memory scrap book)

I have enjoyed walking through life's memories of you on this wonderful journey called life. I tackled this project soon after I was finished with my teaching for the year. I was alone for the day; so I was able to concentrate fully on what was at hand.

As you read this, it is your birthday- your big one- 30 years old- So HAPPY BIRTHDAY! Good heavens, that must mean I am getting older too- I will try not to panic!

As I now recount raising you, I have begun to see some absolute strengths and gifts take shape. I guess it's easier to do this when one begins and ends a project such as this in a short amount of time. Everything comes into focus- Here's what I see:

I see a son with a large capacity to love. You are not hesitant to express your innermost feelings- nor allow the world to flatten your dreams and desires. Where the world has tried to stomp on your spirit- you have pressed forward- always believing there is good in everyone- thus using love and kindness in a world that sometimes only returns it with animosity. As a mother, from this I would want to protect you.

When I watch you laugh and or make me and others laugh, I am reminded of the incredible sense of humor that Jesus has. I believe most people don't associate those words with Him, but I do. You remind me of Him. Yes, I will state that again: You, Josh

Brown, remind me of what my Lord is like. You give me insight into the many facets of our King of Kings.

I see where once stood a blond tassel-haired boy holding Jonny (your favorite bear) in one hand and Ranks (your favorite Threadbare blankie)in the other, all pressed up to your face, now stands a man of remarkable strength, high integrity, great love, a spreader of joy and laughter, extremely brilliant, modest and soft, originator, and seeker of God (and all that He has to give and give and give). Josh, you have barely tapped into all the many blessings the Lord Jesus has in store for you. Remember what I have told you; He has found great delight in you, and with that comes a lifetime of surprises. His favor rests upon you and your family—keep your feelers always at attention; and each day you will see His wonders. I am reminded of the verse from Lamentations: "His compassions never fail. They are new every morning; great is Your faithfulness." Lamentations 3: 22–23

In closing, I want to thank you for allowing me the joy of being your mother. Many times I stand back in awe and wonder on how I could be so blessed to have a son like you. I watch you and am overwhelmed by the GIFT you are to me. Remember to be in constant communion with your Lord- for in a world that is forever changing, regrouping, disappointing, prickly, fast forward speed warping, there is our Jesus who walks BESIDE us- never too busy, never too tired—Thank you thank you thank you for breathing life into a world that is screaming for air.

Your ever grateful mom

It is the Birthday of our Son; and I can barely comprehend the miracle as I stare at you.

Happy Birthday Christopher Brownerella-

The day you were born stands out like it was just a short time ago, but I look at you and it tells me it was longer.

Then the memories begin spreading out- and like a child's water-colored painting, suddenly all the colors begin spilling into others-with everything running together. It's so strange how memories run. But there are those 'memory paintings' that are permanently etched in my heart. Let's go check them out, okay?

I remember begging to hold you when you were born; I had to wait and wait. I remember holding you as I stood in front of a mirror and whispering the words "This is my baby." I would hold your face close to mine.

I remember bike rides to Powderhorn Park—you with your little legs walking around the park, those little arms bent.

I remember how you'd play with so much creativity, especially with the Fisher Price Airport and Adventure people. We can't forget those magic tricks.

Tedderoni (your favorite bear) and brine shrimp, boy scouts, race car derby, hamsters, computer club, and fishing. And we cannot forget all our trips, listening to your marvelous teaching tapes and fun DVDs when we'd arrive at the hotels.

Seems silly to attempt to fragment your life down to a mere page or two, but perhaps it does a mom pleasure to re-visit past moments. Does it do yours as well?

So, on your 38th birthday, I pray you continue to experience all that Jesus has wrapped up for you. Watch for it; keep your eyes and heart open for the tiny packages as well as the big ones. He loves to shower gifts on His children. Christopher Brown, don't you agree we serve a most EXTRAVAGANT GOD?

You have made me a proud mom over and over and over again. Thank you for giving to me my strongest of needs in my love language: TIME. Thank you for always making me feel respected, validated, and worthy. Thank you, my son, for giving to me the most beautiful gift I could ever have dreamed to be given, that of being your mother. You are way too unbelievable to be real. I love you so.

All my love,
Mom

I JUST WANT YOU TO KNOW
Written to my Precious son, Christopher
Gregory Brown- Feb 27, 2009

———❧———

I have wanted for some time to write to you before you get married. I was in Hallmark the other day and found just the perfect gift for you. It is, therefore, the launching pad for this letter. Being a mom with tears that come easily, I realize I am setting myself up for an emotional deluge, but sometimes tears are the door to the heart- So sit back and reminisce with me life as your mother looks back.

REMEMBER

I remember begging to hold you for the first time. Waiting seemed like an eternity. Then they brought you to me. Can heaven be any better than this!

I remember watching you play 'people' and your Fisher Price airplane on the steps of our Chaska tri-level home.

I remember our bike rides to the park. I'd strap you into your little seat that was attached to my bike-and off we'd go to Powderhorn Park. I didn't know life could be so good.

I remember magic shows, home built rockets in the park-and how you'd launch them and we'd look up to see where they'd land.

I remember matching flannel pajamas I'd sewed for you and your brother, Josh. I recall your returning from a day at high school and you'd relax on the recliner with a snack, then you would take a short nap.

I remember Cub Scouts, fish aquariums, dry ice, Thumper (your white bunny), long talks, seeing your eyes well up when I would cry, watching you perform Annie at the high school, you and your tux with the blue satin cummerbund, your gorgeous voice and all the concerts your dad and I were privileged to attend.

But mostly, if I were to choose any of the moments of the past- it would be a memory that is ongoing even today-that of your steady, unwavering, gentle, peaceful, focused, uncompromising faith. For what was evidenced so strongly as a child, has now grown in depth and in even greater understanding.

My Brownerella, you have always owned a large room in my heart. When I look at you, I see so much of me; I feel so much of me. It is so very true what they say: 'To have a child is to decide forever to have your heart go walking around outside your body.'

Now the time has come for me to watch the fruit of my prayers come to pass. Oh I have prayed so very hard for this moment in your life. I cry tears of great joy and gratitude to a God whose timing is always perfect.

Christopher Brownerella, my boy, my love, just always know that I will forever be your biggest Cheerleader- my love for you will go with me into eternity-for you are and will always be the apple of my eye.

Your life now begins. It is not a new chapter, it is a new book- and I am ever so grateful to the Lord for each and every page that you, Shelly Girl and Jesus will write.

In closing, my son, I want you to always look on this little gift as a reminder of our mother/son memories- past, present and future. Now I give you my utmost blessing for a future wrapped and saturated in much laughter and love.

With all my love, Mom

THE DEDICATION OF THE TWINS
My Dearest Josh and Judy:
(March 21st, 2010) written for the
dedication of their twin sons

—⁓—

You know the older I get, the more I realize how very much I have to learn. There is so much I've yet to master; there's so much I've yet to understand about Jesus. But there are some things I DO KNOW. I know when it comes to Godly—'I will teach our children about Jesus'—kind of parents- you both will soar to heights of glory—I also know that even before time began, He chose you to be the specific parents for His own specific children. No one else could give to these two little lambs better than what you both have to give.

Today, as you both dedicate your babies to Jesus, making a promise to point them in the direction of his arms of love, grace, mercies and joys, it is my prayer that as time passes, and as your boys grow, you will often recall this day. Remember, you are not the only ones with a promise. Our Lord makes a promise to you both as well- He will always be intertwined in your parenting- sweetly, gently and lovingly speaking to you words of wisdom, patience, peace and gratitude. All He asks is that you INCLUDE Him in EVERYTHING. As you do, you will actually see your babies take on a reflection of their Heavenly Father's. Because of YOUR nurturing, they will begin to feel His love through YOUR arms, YOUR touch, YOUR whispers of love. It's all about teamwork. Isn't that neat?

I love you both dearly, and am ever so blessed to actually live to see you, my son, Josh- whom I once dressed in a long white baptismal gown, now dedicating your own babies to Jesus. What a blessed grandma I am- oh Jesus is so good.

God's Mighty, Powerful and Extravagant Love be Yours Forever!

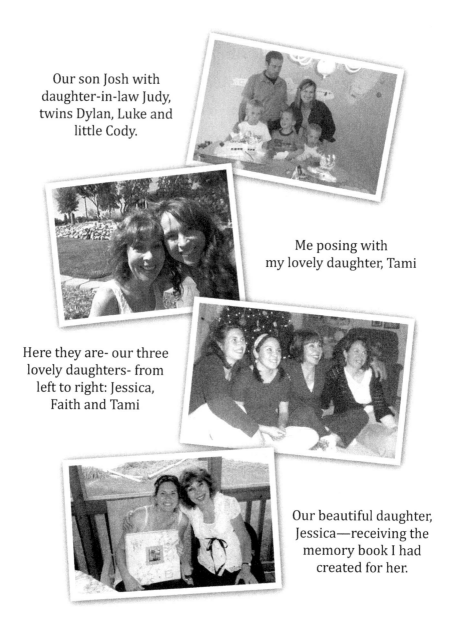

Our son Josh with daughter-in-law Judy, twins Dylan, Luke and little Cody.

Me posing with my lovely daughter, Tami

Here they are- our three lovely daughters- from left to right: Jessica, Faith and Tami

Our beautiful daughter, Jessica—receiving the memory book I had created for her.

A PRAYER FOR MY CHRISTOPHER

Dear Lord Jesus- May the fragrance of this oil be a reminder to my Chris of your presence, your provision, your protection; and that as I anoint my son, I pray that You will give Him everything needed to accomplish all that you desire him to do through his life.

Lord Jesus I thank You for the beauty of Your Holy Spirit that lives so vibrantly in Chris's life. May he always hear Your voice and be sensitive to Your leading each and every day of His life.

Christopher, my precious son, I pray you always will remember this day, and recall it to mind may years from now. Remember his promises are truly new every morning. He will never ever leave you- Your name is branded on His heart for eternity.

Happy Birthday, my son- Remember I love you dearly,
Mom

May this oil be as a healing ointment on each area of his life that needs soothing refreshment.

Happy Birthday Jessica! (2013)

We are in the lovely month of June, and I have just completed your special memory scrapbook album. As I worked away on it, my thoughts would wander to what I wanted to say in the introductory letter. There is so much my heart wants you to know. The trick comes in accurately transferring the 'heart thoughts' to 'written words.' The following is my attempt.

There is much that goes into this album. There is much that goes through me while creating this album. For as a mother begins the rewind process, taking her at warp speed back to when her child was newly born, a strange occurrence takes place within her heart—she begins to actually go back into time and relive many of those past feelings—almost forgetting the current place and time—but re-living a past life—known to us all as: REMEMBER WHEN'S. Unlike the other albums I have made, yours was unusual in that I saw you while I was midstream in creating it. I recall attending the girl's dance recital, and in seeing you, saw a woman. I saw a busy wife and mother when just a few minutes before I had spent hours peering into the eyes of a little girl who liked her Barbies, Care Bears, and Strawberry

Shortcake. I remember just staring at you and wondering where the time flew off to?

The adventure I take throughout the making of your book can be quite an emotional roller coaster ride. I am laughing at a darling Easter Bunny letter you'd written, then finding myself suddenly crying over a heartfelt letter you'd painfully etched— having entrusted your heart with mine.

So, dear daughter, Jessica, I invite you to step into a past dimension known to us all as "childhood". Stay alert to possible tender moments mixed with smiles of joy.

It is your story and no one else has one just like it. It is an original and never possible to be duplicated! Like the snowflakes that fall to earth individually unique, so your life story is presented the same way—I hope you will enjoy each and every page. It is my work of love for you.

With all my love,
Mom

SHELLY GIRL'S BABY SHOWER
(Saturday, May 21st 2011)

———∽∽∽———

My Dear Sweet Shelly Girl, it seems like such a short time ago that I was standing here, telling you how much I loved you and welcoming you into the family. We laughed, we cried, we enjoyed a meal, you opened gifts and talked of your honeymoon plans. You and Chris proved to us all that through prayers, dreams can indeed come true.

Now here I stand—once again praising the Lord for yet another miracle in the making. This one does not involve an upcoming trip, nor a flowing white bridal gown and stunning red roses. Instead, it will come wrapped quite differently; for this will last a lifetime and continue into eternity. It is the one gift in life that we can actually take with us to heaven. For as a toddler's jelly-stained fingerprints can often be found on windows and mirrors- so a mother's fingerprints will always remain on a child's heart—never to be washed away by the world's distractions and intensions. Sometimes it may seem that all efforts are wasted and valueless—but never believe that. Our Lord Jesus will walk (and sometimes run) alongside you throughout your parenting journey. Remember sweetheart, if the Lord's fingerprints remain on you (and they do) then they will most assuredly remain on your child.

Shelly Girl- parenting is one job that a parent cannot do without the intervention of the Lord Himself. There will be exhausting days, lonely days, but also days when your child will do or say something that will make you feel you are experiencing a moment in heaven. One day will never be like another- and if you can force yourself to see your life from God's perspective, you have gained more than I can put into mere words.

As you continue to carry this new life within you-beneath your heart, remember sweetheart- you are partnering with your King-in creating God's most miraculously magnificent miracle, fashioned after God's own heart.

So walk proudly, walk humbly, walk rejoicing that you will wear the most beautiful title in the whole wide world—Mommy!

I love you dearly, my Shelly Girl

Dee

HAPPY BIRTHDAY TO MY BOY

—◦◦◦—

Happy Birthday to my boy- my Josh Krosh (thank you for allowing me to call you that, even after you are all grown up)

I want to give you something that cannot be purchased from a store- nor can it be returned- you cannot wear it, nor use it to work in the yard. It is not a tangible product, but it is alive. Have you guessed it yet? Well it is some words birthed from your mother's heart to you. I hope you will find them uplifting, enlightening and a blessing to your spirit.

My Precious son, my Joshua: 29 years ago today you arrived into our hearts and arms. You were absolutely large and gorgeous. Grammie Brown stated that you looked "like a little Greg". (I could see some of me too!) You were so worth everything that a mother has to do in birthing a child; and so I held you and thanked our Lord for your life.

Then there came crawling, walking and eventually biking on your low riders that you yourself designed. (I wish you would have saved one of them). There were micro-machines and bargaining with your fellow classmates, selling Halloween candy (all laid out at school like a candy store)—the teacher was not at all amused! There were girls, and break ups, road trips (in a most unusual van) with a buddy of yours. But what really stands out to me is a life-changing event that occurred with a Christ-centered organization known as Tec (Teens Encounter Christ). It was all in His plan for you. Like the seasons that follow one another, one day a beautiful "SUNSHINE" began to shine in your life. Her name was Judy, and she had the most unique gift to sparkle and smile and make everyone in the room feel so special. I could barely believe she was for real. But Jesus knew she was real and gave her to you as your sweet lifetime partner. I was so happy for you, and I hugged you and thanked the Lord for this gift.

A too-good-to-be-true wedding followed with a new home, gardening, a love for flowers, veggie gardens (weedless- you are a perfectionist) trees, shrubs and beauty all around you. Could your life be any more blessed? I guess so, for on May 4th 2009, two- not one- but two new unspeakably gorgeous new beauties came splashing into yours and Judy's lives. You tenderly peered at them from their newborn bassinets, first one and then the other. I cried as I stared at you in awe and wonder- my baby boy- now a daddy- way too much to embrace . And I held you, kissed you, congratulated you and cried.

So, my precious son, on this 29th birthday- I just want to say that having you for my son has brought me to rooms in heaven that I would never have even stepped into had you not been born. Thank you for laughter, thank you for your time- thank you for showing to me what a life looks like when it completely is owned and operated by Jesus. You are my boy-my son- my gift- And I hug you, kiss you, congratulate you, and thank the Lord for you. Happy Birthday.

Love, Mom

LIFESONG (WRITTEN TO MY CHILDREN)

—◇◇◇—

Some people say that we each have our own individual smells. That would make sense- because we all have our own individual style- in colors, perfume scents, clothing, books we read, foods we eat, music we listen to, churches we attend. The list goes on and on. Let's face it, we are unique- because our God is creative and never makes the same thing twice.

Okay, with that being said, I began to think of what we would sound like to God if we were put to music, which started me thinking . What would your lifesong sound like? Please keep in mind that each one who comes in contact with you may hear a few different notes. We all resonate a different pitch.

But from my perspective, this is what I believe our Lord Jesus hears as you perform in your bandshell.

At first, there was the ever so soft tinkling of tiny bells, as if gently telling the world, "Look I am here- and because of my existence on the earth, the world will never be the same!" The sound of rushing waters surround you- as you plow into your world with all the gusto a child could claim. Occasionally, if one listens closely, there is an ever soft whisper of tears falling on cotton pillowcases, (soft gentle tears that only your Maker can detect)- but soon, as you grow in beauty, grace and stature, there is a new melody, beginning softly then increasing, like the crescendo of a thousand instruments played in perfect unity. Drums are added and occasional cymbals take their place as well. When someone finds their way right to the very heart of God's, there is an actual personal and authenticated orchestra- Let the drums roll, and trumpets blast. With your new life in Christ, comes the comforting sound of the softness of a waterfall. Because you live in a fallen world, bagpipes and violins occasionally sweep through, but, because you are you, those instruments are once again quickly replaced by the joyous sounds of a fluttering flute. Of course, one day's instruments are never the same as the next; but if one were to look back and combine the days, their music Would all blend into a heavenly ensemble.

My precious children, my prayed for babies—now grown——your music fills not only earth with its harmonious pleasures, but rises to His throne room and angels dance with each endearing chord you strike. If you listen ever so closely, you may be able to hear your Conductor's Voice whispering ever so sweetly, "My children, keep playing your instruments, singing your OWN song, for you are music to My ears."

All my love,
Mom

"I have proclaimed the good news of righteousness in the great assembly; Indeed, I do not restrain my eyes, oh Lord You Yourself know. I have not hidden your righteousness within my heart; I have declared Your faithfulness and salvation. I have not concealed Your lovingkindness and Your truth from the great assembly" (Ps. 40: 9–10 NKJV).

TO ALL THE LITTLE GIRLS AND THEIR DADDIES

—⁕—

I remember standing quite precariously a few short feet in front of my daddy. He would say when, then I, (with my back to him and I was not allowed to peek)- would fall into his waiting arms. Its sounds simpler than it was. For some strange reason, I feared he would not be able or ready to catch me. It was so difficult to not see those strong outstretched ever-ready arms. Yet, as we did this over and over, I began to feel secure; he had proven himself trustworthy- I so learned I had absolutely nothing to fear.

Dads, for just a moment, I would like you to envision yourselves in that same picture frame. There you are, standing behind your daughter, strong arms outstretched, ready to catch her, ready to prove yourselves over and over again- that you will be there. You will be present when she falls back, present when she is so exuberant she can barely speak, present when the tears keep falling,(and what you want most is to just be able to take the pain away), present to believe in her when she thinks no one else does. Dads, speaking from the viewpoint of a daughter myself- your lovely girl may very well see herself from the eyes of her daddy. And when the world starts trying to prove her eyes wrong, please be there to remind her that she will always be your princess.

Dads- you have been given a job you cannot do alone. Some have tried, and from the outside, it may look like they are succeeding but, not really. Our Lord Jesus so desires to come alongside you- prompting you; for we are like children in a school play, forgetting our lines, needing outside assistance.

In conclusion, I want you to take a moment and look at your lovely daughter. Read her eyes; for they have the ability to say more than words ever could. And when this evening closes and you pick up the traditions of life where you left them, please remember this time- a short moment in time, when the two of you shared something that can never be repeated in just the same way- and know that you have planted a seed that will last a lifetime. Please remember to water it, treat it tenderly. I promise you that seed will grow into the most gloriously beautiful flower you can ever imagine—bringing you great joy and blessings.

In the words of Joseph Addison "Certain is it that there is no kind of affection so purely angelic as of a father to a daughter. In love to our wives there is desire; to our sons, ambition, but to our daughters, there is something which there are no words to express." 3

Happy Mother's Day—

If only you could see the beauty of your own individual mothering quilt. Oh you would smile and you would run your fingers over all the various textures. Look at that frolicy gingham square full of goofiness and giggles, smiles threaded into each square. Oh, and run your fingers over the velvet piece, so soft and tender, healing to the touch. There are darker squares as well, to remind you that we cannot mother on our own strengths; but we need to continuously lean on our Lord Jesus. Gaze into the bright morning-sun yellows; they have been patched in throughout the quilt. Some are large squares, some small - to remind you that mothering can have unplanned spontaneous moments of laughter throughout a given week, if we are open to them. Some of the squares are pure linen white, still to be colored. I cannot wait to see what you and Jesus will create! Happy quilting.

IN HONOR OF TAMI ON HER SURPRISE BIRTHDAY PARTY

(9–16–09)

—❧—

MY HERO

I lay in bed this morning trying to find the right words for my daughter as I see her. Several words came to mind- but just did not seem to fit. Then it came- and I knew I could not find any better word that defines our relationship.

Now I realize that the tables should be turned in this area- and in actuality, that reminds me of the day Heaven came down to meet me. Tami's assignment in one of her classes in school was to write about a person they admire, and then bring them to class and share with them all their attributes. As I sat in that classroom listening, I felt it to be surreal; and then when I was convinced it could not get better, she played the song, "The Wind Beneath My Wings," by Bette Middler. I never forgot that. But, many years have passed and much water over that bridge. I am here today to say to you, beautiful daughter, that you are my Hero and the Wind Beneath My Wings!

Thoughts run through my mind that this sounds unhealthy or not normal. It's 'supposed to be' the other way around. But 'supposed to be' is not my reality- and I cannot live my life on the need to be, try to be, and should be—it is what it is - and if this is wrong or put into the category of the most widely used word in the human language these days, 'disfunctional,' then I am indeed the guilty party—let it be written, then let it be said.

I guess it all breaks down to how you define the word: 'Hero.' Here is how I define it. To me, a hero is someone who works toward the mission God has called them to be and do. They are always steadfastly pointed to that goal. Tami, as we all know, God has called you out among the rest to walk toward His calling for you in many areas. But the one I am blessed with is just this: You are able to 'call someone out' of their God given gifts and bring them to the realization- to the light- and provide them with the belief in themselves that they can do great things. I have seen you do this to countless souls; I am not the only one to be blessed by your calling.

So Tami, I thank you for being a Hero to me- for releasing in me what may have been shackled by man's wrong teachings. Now I am free to be just who I am. You accept people for where they are, and even encourage that freedom by your own example of transparency (I love that word) and realness. You have unlocked my chains and I love you.

You are my Hero- and I make no apologies. Happy Birthday Beauty Queen.

Love,

Mom

NOT IN MY SUNDAY BEST
Wed. July 21st 2010

—◦◦◦—

Wow Jesus- You are so not into outward appearance. There I was, unshowered- work clothes- no make-up- working to get ready for the Beautiful Girls BBQ I had planned months before; then a friend of Faith's began talking about her dreams- one spirited story led to another- and like stepping stones leading to a field of wild poppies, we basked in the fragrance of all You are giving to this young woman. We prayed and saw this time ending in a victorious breakdown of generational strongholds and enlightenment on all Your gifts you are giving to her and to me. Your vessel, on the outside looking like a work woman. I was so NOT IN MY SUNDAY BEST.

A SENSE OF WELL BEING

(July 10)

(the morning after the BBQ
with the Beautiful girls)

—◦◦◦—

Have you ever experienced it?—It's like all is right with the world- you're at peace. You feel grateful to the Lord you have things to look forward to- and a relief to have something that you worked hard to accomplish now finished. You are comfortable with who you are- like the wheel is slowing turning and you are one of the spokes. Peace peace peace - I wish I could always feel this way.

BRING YOUR KEYS

(Sept. 3, 2010)

—⁓—

I t was an exciting time. We were meeting my sister, Dawn, her friend, and her daughter Leah, and renting a cabin on the lake. I had everything planned- complete with a special writing I had written and Bible verses I had chosen. I wanted to pray over the 3 of them as well. I felt ever led to anoint them. I had checked it out with Jesus and He was thumbs up on it. I had packing to do and the day sped by. The morning we were to leave, I'd gotten up at 4:00 AM- woke Faith and Greg—and scampered to and fro as one does to prepare for a trip. But as I was getting ready to leave, I heard a sweet voice in my spirit say, "Bring your keys." I paused, wondering why I should bring my keys. I thought maybe it was because Greg might misplace his and we would be locked out of the car. I really did not know, but I obeyed. That evening, as we were all gathered around the cabin table, I felt it was a great time to have my little inspirational time. I read my writing- and the Bible verses. Then I stopped dead in my tracks—for though I had planned to anoint them, I had forgotten to pack the oil. Wait - I had listened to the Holy Spirit's nudging- the anointing oil had been attached to my keys! Ah, that's why I was to bring them! As I proceeded to pray and anoint each one, I could not help but feel Jesus blessing my humble attempts. It was truly His way of approving my plan.

"The very steps we take are from God; otherwise how would we know where we are going?" Proverbs 20: 24 The Message Bible

THE WORLD OF THE UNDERSTATED- WHERE LESS IS MORE

—⟨⟨⟨⟩⟩⟩—

I am thinking of the beauty of small, less, and quiet- One rose is equally if not more lovely as 3 dozen. Sometimes the less words spoken have the greatest impact. The less furniture in a home makes for a bigger look to the house. Too much make-up can work reverse and make a woman look older. In a world of overabundance, excessive and overkill lifestyles, I find a refreshment in less, simple and understatements. There is beauty in less.

THE PHONE CALL
(Dec. 22, 2010)

I was depressed- crying and asking Jesus for a favor- 'Could you please pick someone today who could call me and cheer me up; but if You choose not to, I will be okay too.' The hours passed and I busied myself making 'bars in a jar' gifts for the family. Then the phone rang; It was my sister, the perfect choice. He had once again taken care of my heart.

THE BAPTISM
(April 21st, 2011)

—⟨∾∾⟩—

I remember reading the e-mail from Clara- 'There will be a special baptism and communion service on Thursday night-please join us.' I felt a gentle stirring in my spirit. I fought it and would vacillate. Then Tami told me Rachel, my granddaughter, was getting baptized. I did not want to miss out on this blessing-so I e-mailed Clara to say I was coming; There, now it was official. But I felt a nudging- like He was encouraging me to do this as well. I was nervous but excited. I had decided to get baptized because of my dream and the new depth of my walk He was taking me on. The dream was way back in March. I had been dreaming about babies quite frequently. The dream centered around some party event. Tami and Matt were in charge of games and called everyone outside. I was carrying this baby and had an urgency to feed it. As I was carrying it, the baby spoke like an adult and said, "I'm done with this." I then found a sofa to sit down. As

Tami and Matt directed games, I fed my baby. When I picked up the baby to burp it, it became a big girl of 12 or 13 years old. I had interpreted the dream to mean I am that baby and I am done with the baby food and baby steps of my spiritual walk- I am ready for the meat. I am ready to grow up in the things of the prophetic. "I will sing a new song to You, Oh God. On a harp of 19 strings I will sing praises to You." (Ps. 144:9 NKJV).

Now, back to the baptism. Rachel, Faith(my daughter) and I were in the bathroom. Rachel and I were getting ready- when Faith mentioned she too was feeling she should get baptized— awesome! Pastor Sam had talked about what may happen- he mentioned old childhood pains and thought processes may come tumbling down. Well, when it was my turn (right after Rachies), Pastor Sam said, "Ok- who's next?" I stepped forward. As I climbed the steps, (this was a printing press ink tub), I was crying and said to Pastor Sam, "This is so emotional."—to which Sam replied, "That's good." He then looked at me and said, "Oh so you're the one." As he placed his hand on me, he prayed, "Dee- you have been told a stack of lies as a child- that is broken as of now. You are set free and you are a new person in Jesus." He then lowered me completely under the water. As I came up, I held my arms up high and made a sign with my arms that it is done, fin- ished, past cancelled. Later, we all had communion. Jesus- Holy Spirit- I feel new- renewed and see more clearly. Thank you for that experience. Now take my hand and show me how to live a healthy Dee. Amen!

ANALOGY

I am going deeper. Jesus and I are scuba diving- He gently and lovingly says to me, "Dee, come deeper- the fish are even more lovely and colorful the deeper you go!"

JUST FOR SHOW
(June 5, 2011)

―⁓―

When I was growing up in our upstairs farmhouse flat, I heard the words, "That's just for show," more times than I could tell you. "Don't use that towel, it's just for show, don't lay on that pillow, it's just for show." When I grew up and had a home of my own, I too found myself doing the same thing and using the same expression: 'JUST FOR SHOW'——'Don't use that towel it's just for show, please don't lay your head on that pillow because it's just for show.' Even my watch I wear on Sundays doesn't work. It doesn't tell time; but I wear it anyway because it looks nice. But it is, in fact, just for show. This is all fine and good, but I got to thinking about us as people- our lives, our words, our actions. How much is just for show? Let me explain:

When we listen to a friend or family member share a hurt of their heart, do we add the necessary and socially acceptable caring nods and then walk away and completely forget we even talked to that person? Or what about all those times we have been asked, "How are you?"- and we unthinkingly and completely out of habit answer, "Just fine,"(because someone we don't know- as well as people we do- might think we're not together that day.)

It's like we carry around a big sandwich sign that reads: "Watch me, listen to me, and you will know that I am always in one piece- put together- fully fashioned- no worries- no cares- for I am,"Just for Show!"

As I see it—and as I age, I tend to want less cargo. I want less baggage; and the yearning to travel light continues to gnaw at me. I love to get rid of unneeded possessions around my home. Giving stuff away, consigning, selling them at a garage sale, clearing out the house and simplifying have become my soap box to friends and family. Like melted chocolate swirled into a vanilla cake batter, this "simplicity thing" has swirled its way into my personality as well. I have seen my realness and transparency played out. I will tell you I no way miss the heavy and burdensome stuff that I once carried in my pockets. This stuff had names: showiness, imposters, emptiness, surface talk . It's so refreshing to leave that behind- and instead run through a child's summer sprinkler- with my arms held wide- knowing I am free and I am not "Just For Show!"

WHAT WE'RE CREATED FOR
(Jan. 20th, 2011)

—⟪⟫—

I believe everyone of us has one strong gift that stands out above the others. If you don't know yours, listen for people to observe it; they will notice it. Many times we don't see it- but others do. Still, if you don't hear it from others, here is a sure-fired way: You will feel an indescribable joy doing it—a feeling of purpose will flood over you-a peaceful kind of joy- like you are doing exactly what you are made for. Here is my story:

It was Tuesday- I saw one of my favorite moms at pre-school. Though her child is not in my class, I had been drawn to the fabulous spirit in this woman. So when I saw her come, I announced, "Oh, there's our sunshine, now the day can begin!" After she had deposited her daughter into her classroom, I caught her as she was leaving. I put my arm around her and said, 'You see, when Jesus forms a person, He places sunshine and joy in some- not many who walk this earth have it- but you do; and it is so needed, —so let your sunshine show. The world will forever try to squash it. Don't let it- for you are so needed to brighten up the world and the lives of His people.' As I spoke, she became teary and said, "Yes, that is just what is happening now." Then she said she would remember that- and that this has made her day.

I then walked back into my pre-school room feeling more fulfilled than I had felt in many months.

THESE RECURRING "BABY" DREAMS
(June 5, 2011)

—✿—

I have had around 4 or 5—each one spaced a couple months apart. Now, last night another one- I am carrying around this baby (but the baby has not been born yet)- still I am looking at this baby and concerned- I don't want it to get sick before its born.

I looked up baby in my dream book: new Beginning, new Idea, new work (church).

"Behold, I will do a new thing; now it shall spring forth (new birth)- shall you not know it? I will even make a way in the wilderness and rivers in the dessert" (Isa. 43:19 NKJV).

A CRACKED VESSEL-
HIS FAVORITE KIND

———ᴗᴗᴗ———

I t was Friday- June 10ᵗʰ 2011. I had just arrived at the church to help with our Pre-school garage sale. I noticed my friend talking to a woman who was shopping at our sale. She was Telling her she prays and asks God to help her not to worry; and the woman was curious how to do that. I proceeded to walk past them. I laid my purse in the kitchen- then I heard my name: My friend called me over and asked about the book: 'Jesus Calling.' I walked over and told her. The woman looked very interested and ever so ripe for Jesus. I asked her if I could pray for her. She readily said, "Yes, yes!" I led her to the back table and quickly set up 2 chairs. I clasped her hands in mine and I prayed for her. When I had finished, she was teary and ever so child-like, asking questions like: "How did you do that? How did you learn that?" She had so many questions. Jesus gave me the answers; so for the next hour, Jesus used me to minister to her. When we were finished, I noticed not one shopper had come through the church doors—the Lord had kept them all away- giving us total privacy. As we concluded, the shoppers started coming. What a morning—I felt like, "This is what I am made for, Jesus!" Thank you for finding me worthy to lead my first person to You. Though I am a cracked vessel, You told me that those are your best kind You like to use. I shall continue to pray for this woman and her son.

BEYOND THE NEST

(June 27, 2011)

———❧———

Every spring God hands us a package wrapped in a bundle, commonly known as: 'a bird's nest with eggs.' We have 4 hanging baskets on our veranda. And early spring is the time that the House Finches find their way to our baskets. There are usually around 4 or 5 eggs. And every other day, I gingerly lift the basket down, water the flowers, and replace it on its hook. Of course, the female bird chirps on a nearby tree, as I do my dastardly deed- but soon she returns. When they hatch, it is always exciting- as we once more marvel at the majestic detailing of His world. Now, today, as I tapped on the base of the planter and began lifting it down, I witnessed 4 heavenly winged angels flying to a nearby tree. I had been blessed to actually see their exit from their little safety net- the nest where their lives began. I gazed as their small new wings carried them.

Isn't this like our own lives? We are ecstatic to learn of new life on the way. We prepare. We have even borrowed the word from our feathered friends: "nesting"- meaning preparing for the arrival. The baby is born- and the eggs have hatched. Then there is much busy-ness as new life is cared for, nourished and nurtured. Then, when these wings are strong enough- we encourage them to fly. As their wings mature, so does their height, speed and distance. They are free; for there is some deep down yearning for the 'something more' that is out there—no longer content to sit quietly under a veranda roof in a hanging basket. Somehow that fledgling wants to leave all that is known to explore all that is unknown; and they are right, there is so much more!

Life is full of wondrous surprises- still, there remains a pattern- We have and we release. Most of us are blessed with an overabundance of blessings in a lifetime. All of us know the pain of releasing—that of allowing and even encouraging our loved ones to use their wings—I did and found immeasurable peace in so doing. Someday soon my loved ones will release me into the arms of the One who guided me through my own life's flight.

THE WINDOW
(July 16, 2011)

—•••—

S eems like there are certain words or expressions each one of us latch on to and repeat over and over again; it's like we take ownership of them—those words that become popular for the 'season' (there's one right there!) words such as: hosed, bug, you betcha (here's a super favorite: awkward!)-oh, 'super'—that's one too! Then there's: dysfunctional, boundaries, here's the situation, and we cannot forget: unbelievable, profound, beyond, my dear, the bottom line, not so much, perfect. I am sure you could fill in a few yourself. But here is mine: WINDOW! This word is absolutely most appropriate in my vocabulary so much of the time.

In life, it seems there are pockets of time (there's another one)or windows, when certain actions or well chosen words work best—it's like the situation is almost screaming out to us: "Use me now! Do this now!" Oh sure, one can always blurt out or act on a situation whenever one feels like it, but the most effective, most powerful and memorable are the words and actions performed in the arena of that WINDOW. Here is how it works: first I pray about what to say or do, which subsequently alerts me to that ripe moment—and it does come—then we have the choice to recognize it, hold on to it, and make a difference, or to pass it by as one would through a flowerbed, not picking a single flower.

The next time you pray about the when and what of a situation, be on guard for the 'window' He shows you. Then hold it and go for it. You will be pleasantly pleased in the results.

"A word fitly spoken is like apples of gold in settings of silver." (Prov. 25:11 NKJV)

GOD'S PAINTBRUSH

A PRAYER AND REVELATION (Aug 8, 2011),

—◦◦◦—

I am currently in a time of my life that Your paintbrush becomes very evident to me- splashing bold colors—specifically painting the days with your own handiwork. And it is not just days, but actual seasons, when I fall back, mouth open in wonder of your timing . Oh yes You have been here. You have been caught, for your brush strokes give You away- giving clear evidence of Your detailed care for me.

I am in transition- one of the loves of my life (taking up much of my heart room) is moving away from me. I have struggled immensely, cried profusely, and felt waves of grief that would rise and fall, rise and then fall. But I suddenly realized some brush strokes (circumstances) that have given You away; and I realize You are painting this picture for me—like finding out my dear friend is enrolling her daughter in my pre-school class, which means I have the absolute and show-stopping pleasure of seeing her quite frequently throughout the school year. This person, as You know, is a huge blessing to me—a Sentry of my Heart. It was so You Jesus. Then, as is the as this is the actual week of their departure, I suddenly noticed how You have filled my calendar, especially next week—with good stuff and events to look forward to. I realize something. Your paint brush at work, once again keeping me busy and stimulated. You know me—that to be alone right at this time would be unhealthy—You know me so well that You would bring my friend into my school days- to remind, embrace, lift and carry me. I stand in awe of all your colorful supernatural splendor! Amen.

THE DEPARTURE

(Aug. 14, 2011)

—◦◦◦—

Yesterday I had to do something that I had been anticipating and dreading for exactly four months. It was on April 13th that Matt, my son in law, had announced he would be moving his family to Redding, California to pursue his vocation change- that of returning to school to be a Christian counselor. I first went into a form of trauma- not being able to react, then shaking, then crying. I have replayed in my mind memories of virtually everything I did with Tami, Matt and my four grandchildren. I wrote about it, cried about it and prayed about it. I presented them with farewell gifts. At 3:00 PM on August 13, Greg, Faith and I stood in Matt's parent's home and said our good-byes. I watched as Greg cried, telling Tami that Minneapolis is losing a light; but Redding is gaining one. I recall telling Tami that I delight in her. We prayed, then left. Jesus, I know Your strong arms were holding me up. Because of You, I remained in control.

Because of You, I am not heartsick. Because of You, I have hope. Thank you, Jesus for not letting me crash and burn. I am amazed by You! Jesus, please don't ever let go of me.

THE SAFETY NET
(Sept- 2011)

—⁓—

Did you ever experience an off day? This is a day when you feel that as hard as you try, you cannot walk a straight line. Recently, I lived such a day. I remember how it began. I was driving Faith, my youngest daughter, to school. I happened to see two high school kids waiting for the bus, so I waved to them. They glared grimly at me as I drove past them. I felt rejected and stupid. Little did I know that it would be a foretaste of how the rest of the day and evening would go. That evening, as I sat at my desk in my pre-school room during our open house, I called out to Jesus for help. Within minutes, I was visited by a mom and a former student—then was joined by two more as well. This pumped me back up; they had so many words of encouragement. As I got in my car that evening, I whispered, "Thank you, Jesus." Little did I know that within a day and a half, I would be in a similar deflated state, feeling devalued and worthless—so I drove over to the Christian bookstore near my home. I am friends with the owner. We share our hearts. I tear up (I always do when she and I talk). She shows me the new loft upstairs. She tells me her dream is being fulfilled (which is to have a meeting place for people to come). Then this lovely woman walks in, who will be starting up next door with this gathering place for women. She and the owner are all excited about what Jesus is doing in their lives. So the three of us are standing there talking; I say, 'You know I love to see His fingerprints in our lives show up. He is right here in the middle of it all.' Then I pressed my finger on the counter top. They all agreed and were equally encouraged. Then I went on to say, ' As we walk along our lifepath, God places flowers interspersed. We pick them and know He has deliberately placed them there- to encourage us along the way.' At that point, this woman, Suzy, asks if I journal. I told her that I am in the middle of writing a book. She asks if I have ever taught a journaling class. I answer, 'Yes. I taught a Creative Writing Class of 6th, 7th, and 8th graders.' She then asks if I would pray about teaching a group of women how to journal. She hands me literature on it. I ask Jesus and it seems He says, "Yes, yes"—almost before I can barely get the question out to Him. So I leave- pumped back up all over again.

And as I ponder both these events, I cannot help but see before my eyes a safety net, like the kind we see in a circus.

So here we all are, doing life—complete with all the acrobatic stunts we are pushed into doing each day-switching from swing to swing, flips, and spins. The swinging never really stops, but because we live in an imperfect world, sometimes we let go of the swing. Whether purposely or haphazardly, we feel ourselves falling, falling, falling. Then we feel beneath us not a rock hard floor, but instead a cushy soft netting. If we look really closely, we discover it isn't netting at all; instead, it is the strong arms of Jesus, whispering softly, "It's Me. I am here. I have been here all along, and I will never let you crash." Thank You, Jesus, for all your faithful catches.

HAPPY BIRTHDAY PRECIOUS ONE OF MINE

(Sept. 16, 2011- written to my daughter on her 37th birthday- now living in Redding- 1st birthday away from home)

---*◈◈◈*---

Happy Birthday Precious one of mine! You are there and I am here- a most distant situation to be in; but the bond we as mother and daughter share far surpasses any and all distances on a silly old map. For there exists in the heart a certain place that neither time nor distance can penetrate. Jesus did His wondrous and powerful work with us long before today became a reality. Our hearts no longer are threatened by those once dreaded enemies (time and distance). When Jesus seals a bond, it is secure for eternity. I am praying you have an awesome day, my girl. I embrace all that you are, for there is much in you to share! I love you so much! Mom

THE MYSTERIOUS FRAGRANCE

(Sept. 30, 2011)

—◦◦◦—

It was around 5:00 PM on a Friday. I had spent the day helping Judy, my daughter in law, and Josh, my son, with the buddies (my 3 grandchildren). Judy was sick from the chemo treatment. On my way home, I picked up Faith, my youngest daughter. As we pulled into our garage, I happened to smell this lovely fragrance, not like anything I had ever smelled. At first I did not know what to think. I loved it. I felt incredible peace. As I got out of the car, the fragrance became even stronger. I proceeded to ask Faith to come stand by me - to see if she could smell it as well. She definitely agreed and mentioned that it sort of smelled like the anointing oil I keep on my key chain. We both thought perhaps the oil had spilled out—but when I checked, the cap was on as tightly as possible. As we walked into the house, the fragrance slowly faded. What was it? An angelic visitation was the first answer that came to me; and I am blown away by His goodness. Thank you Jesus—thank you Sweet Jesus!

THE FRAGRANCE OF
THE HOLY SPIRIT

—⟨⟨∕∕⟩⟩—

The fragrance of the presence of the Holy Spirit- it was like some ancient fragrance- sweet and spicy- though not lingering—quickly gone.

"I am full, having received from Epaphroditus, the things sent from you, a sweet-smelling aroma, an acceptable sacrifice, well pleasing to God." (Phil. 4:18 NKJV)

When one is blessed to be in the presence of God, the Holy Spirit will manifest Himself in different ways. There is like a sweet honey cinnamon-y smell to it, and with it comes a sense of peace and wonderment like nothing else one has ever experienced.

SWEETHEART

(Nov. 4, 2011)

———※※※———

I remember seeing her, serving what ever table she could clean up- always with a smile—zealously working with one goal in mind- to be the best at what and where God had placed her. When she came to our table and asked if she could clear some plates, I looked at her and replied, 'Thanks, sweetheart.' My grandchildren were with me. I guess they heard me call her that and so they too began referring to her as "sweetheart." For a moment, I wondered if they, perhaps, thought that that was her name. Finally, I walked up to her and mentioned that I had remembered her from the last time we were there. I told her she shined much light on the place. She mentioned that all she wanted to do was please the customers and that it was all for the Glory of God. I gave her a final hug as we left.

But I could not help think about all of us- and the jobs that each one of us is called to do. It has challenged me to try to be the best at what I do no matter how humbling that may be. Jesus, You are not so much into—"What we do" but rather how much love we do it in.

ASK AND IT SHALL BE
GIVEN TO YOU
A DIVINE APPOINTMENT (Nov. 9, 2011)

The morning began like every other week-day morning-except during this usually quiet time with Jesus, I had decided to have some fun with it. So I had asked Jesus to bring someone into my life today that I could pray with and counsel.

I then went about my day- took Faith, my youngest daughter, to school- then drove to work. The morning went well; and at 11:30, I proceeded to my next assignment- that of: 'lunch bunch.' It was around 12:15 when a young woman whom I have past mentored walked into the lunchroom, visibly hurting. We hugged her and found out her great grandpa had just passed away. To make it worse, it was her birthday. The other teacher and I prayed for her and tried to comfort her. Eventually, we found ourselves alone. It was then she turned to me and asked, "Dee, can you tell me how to deal with people who continually walk all over me and how to say no to people that keep asking me for favors at work?" Apparently she had taken on other people's duties and they were disrespecting her. Well, I quickly pulled up a chair and began to speak life into her spirit. As I talked, I suddenly remembered the prayer I had prayed earlier that morning. My eyes welled with tears as I shared with her my request earlier that day. I finished with a prayer over her- then proceeded to drive home. I could feel His love shining all around me; And He was smiling. I had asked and He had answered. It was truly a moment in time. I felt so close to my Lord that I could almost have reached out and touched Him. I think it is called: 'divine appointment'—truly a miracle to experience.

THE ANOINTING

(Nov. 18, 2011)

She entered my pre-school room very teary. She guarded her words, "I am praying about stepping out into a position God might be calling me into- but there is so much at stake." I told her that I would love to pray for her and anoint her. We agreed it would be this coming Friday at 8:30 AM. When that morning arrived, we walked into the fellowship hall, sat down, and she began to read to me from her journal. As she read, I realized the Lord had prepared her for this day by telling her she was to be anointed. She looked up at me, with tears in her eyes and said, "Dee, God chose you to be the one- just like Samuel choosing David." I began to cry and cry.

Jesus, most of the time I feel so small and insignificant, not very smart or fancy. Yet, You say in Your Word that You will confound the wise and important and lift up and use the lowly. Thank you. I feel encouraged to be just who I am- because that is who You made me to be. Help me walk in my destiny that You have laid before me.

THOSE 'PAJAMAS AND NO MAKE-UP' FRIENDS

(Wed. Nov 23, 2011)

—⟨ᴓ⟩—

S he called in the morning, saying she would be dropping off some bins of baby clothes. It was my day off and I felt like staying in my pink fleece PJ's. I thought for a moment about our comfort level with various people. I know for family (including daughters-in-law and sons-in-law) pajamas and no make-up surround my comfort zone with them. Why? Perhaps because they know my age—that I am the mother/grandmother figure— no strivings or cover up needed. But then there is that next circle of friends- though I would love to say the same 'comfort' zone applies to them, I cannot. Why? Because they are that group of people that have, perhaps as some point, commented on how good I look, etc. I recall those such words; and I do not want to lose that image. So I humbly admit, realness in this case, loses to 'image.' But is there more? Do I really feel like I need to maintain a certain level of rapport and dignity and what happens if and when I fail? We love to say 'unconditional love' but I walk softly there, still testing those waters. Now, if you will please excuse me, I need to get dressed and apply a few dabs of make-up. She'll be here soon!

"Just as lotions and fragrance give sensual delight, a sweet friendship refreshes the soul." Prov. 27: 9 The Message Bible

Our Dear Friends, Diane and Ron- truly they are the 'Pajama and no make-up' kind of friends. They have been sent as gifts from Jesus to us.

Best Friend, Sally, for 32 years and counting!

Sally and I attending a tea party. Check out our darling straw hats.

A MOTHER'S PARABLE FOR HER SONS
(Dec. 26, 2011)

—◦◦◦—

Once there was a farmer who had been blessed with all the joys his heart could hold- his children were strong, virtuous and of high integrity. Their love for God went deep and full. The farmer also had various cattle, chickens and sheep- all healthy and sturdy.

One day the farmer approached his oldest son and firmly yet lovingly told him what had been on his heart for some time. He was now at a time to give all that mattered, all that really counted, to his son. The son was quite grateful and tears formed in his eyes as he gave his father a hug. After they had exchanged warm words of affection, the farmer stood face-to-face with his son, and, taking his hand, handed him a strange tool. "This is now yours," the father said. "With it, you will be able to accomplish many tasks. You see, though you have been given great honor to have received all that I have, it has not been given to you freely. As with everything," he continued, "it too comes with a price. But I am giving you everything you need to complete our transaction." With that, the farmer took the tool from his son's hand and lovingly explained all the many tasks that it could do. "You see, son," the man began, "The barn for the cattle needs a new roof." He then proceeded to change the tool into a hammer. "And I have needed to repair the fence that holds the chickens in." Again, he took the tool; it became a saw. The son was amazed at all that could be accomplished with this strange yet mighty tool. "The one thing you must remember is that you need to make the effort to pick it up and use it properly. The tool needs you. It will not do the work on its own. It needs you!" After the farmer walked away, the son grasped the tool firmly in his hands. He would determine to maintain, repair and manage the farm; and, eventually, in time, hand this tool to his own son. The tool had been passed—it would not sit idle.

"Point your kids in the right direction, when they're old, they won't be lost." Prov. 22:6 The Message Bible

COME AS YOU ARE

—⟨⟩—

When does it finally, if ever, become comfortable coming as you are?

I mean who can I be around without being decked out in painted face and color-coordinated clothes? And what is it about feeling I need to come to the table with my best dishes, crystal and silver? And when did all this begin? It doesn't stop there either!

It's like I somehow feel I need to prove myself accepted and guaranteed. If I can look my best, then it is all good - and what kind of a price do I pay for such shallow showmanship?

I enjoy the crystal frankness and refreshing transparency in the youth of today. I have also met a microscopic handful of REAL ADULTS as well. They are the people who do not try to make themselves and their lives appear unreal and perfect. These people invite me to be real. It is like they roll out the red carpet for me to boldly, unabashedly, and confidently just be me - no curtains or shades or blinds will be needed. Life is real. Life happens. Thank you, Lord, for all the people who remind me that whether I wear Estee Lauder make-up or Walmart sweats, I am who I am; and I am invited to 'come as you are'!

LIKE A BASKET OF FRUIT

(Jan. 21st, 2012)

—◦◦◦—

Life, with all the possibilities, kindnesses, surprises, and blessings we have at our disposal, we still have a choice to walk away or pick up the banana or grapes out of the basket-and give the much needed nourishment to others; but it is yours To choose, either give it away, or walk away.

LIFE IS TOO SHORT TO WEAR GRAY
(Feb. 21, 2012)

—◈—

As my friend stepped into my home on this sunny February afternoon, she commenced to share her story about the purchase of her new coat. She said she had brought a gray coat Up to the register, when suddenly she received this revelation, "Wait, life's too short to wear gray!" She quickly replaced it with a red one and immediately bought it.

It started me thinking about Carpe' Diem. Yes, they both fall under the same chapter. Do not put off (an encouraging word, kind deed, a prayer, a hug, a touch, a smile, a gift) . If you have the chance, seize it, grab hold of it, run with it - and do not allow yourself to be talked out of it. In the short span of one's life, there is absolutely no room for regrets of the "should have's".

In a world where we are surrounded by stoicism, complacency, ambivalence and silence, even the smallest of compliments will light up people's faces. The human race is screaming for love, reassurance, and a pat on the back. Hasn't there been enough hardened silence and holding back? I am so done with the browns and grays of life. My friend is right, "life IS too short to wear gray!"

ON RECEIVING FLOWERS
(Thursday, April 26, 2012)

—◈—

It is euphoric- a celestial feeling- almost like the world is playing a symphony personally composed in your honor. I feel beautiful, honored, treasured and loved.

I was standing in my pre-school room. I suddenly saw two people standing by me—one of them was holding this gorgeous bouquet of flowers. He said, "Are you Dee?" I said, "Yes." "These are for you," He said with a warm smile. I instantly began crying, saying, "You must love your job!"—he replied, "Yes, I do!" He really got his money's worth with my reaction. I don't know how other people react upon receiving flowers, but I sure know how I do. The Lord had placed this idea into the heart of my husband, Greg, and he had responded in obedience. It was a day of extravagance, tears and cleansing. Thank you Jesus for the flowers.

WHEN GOD LIFTS THE GRACE
Dec. 27, 2011

———《♦》———

I remember hearing my daughter speak of this strange phenomenon. She explained there was such peace and confirmation. Yet I silently had questioned why He would lift such a blessing as this. Now I know.

A few years ago, I felt the need to detach myself from an unpleasantly unhealthy acquaintance. Strangely, I remember feeling a peace and almost lightness in my spirit, with no guilt attached. Now, I find myself in a similar place. It is time to sever, like one would cut a flying stringed balloon. I verbally announced, "I am done!" Instead of a guilt-ridden feeling, I once again felt light, unburdened and free. When I shared it all with Jesus, He Lovingly affirmed my decision, saying, Your job here is done. He had had many opportunities. You are free." The grace had been lifted. There are so many things I have yet to learn of You, Lord

Jesus. But one thing I am assured of, proven over and over, when there is peace that floods my spirit - I know You are in it.

THE ABANDONED NEST

(May 5, 2012)

———〜〜〜———

We had noticed the nest early one spring day. We waited excitedly for the mother bird to fill it. Within days, there she was, a Robin; She had perched peacefully on her throne- yet somewhat ruffled when my daughter would cut the lawn- (evidently a bit too close for comfort around her tree). One day, while she was gone, we peeked in and saw a gorgeous blue egg. We were so excited! Later that afternoon, we had thunderstorms. The following morning I had noticed she was not on her nest- nor was she that afternoon. Later, we painfully discovered the nest was now empty; and two eggs lay broken along the driveway's edge (not far from her nest). Now each morning, the nest remains empty- like an abandoned dwelling, where once was life. Perhaps the storm was too powerful- and blew the eggs out from its safety net. What happened to the mother- that she could not have protected the eggs from the storm? Whatever the case, I pray that You, Jesus, will protect me from the storms. And when the storms do come, You will give me the courage to never abandon my post. My nest is in You; hold it secure—keep me warm and safe—and help me to stay the course.

THE DREAM
(August 23, 2012)

—✺—

It had been a hard week. I felt like every step I walked was facing against the wind. Anxiety attacks continued to plague me- and depression loomed like a dark cloud. Then my daughter called, saying she had a dream about me last night. In it, we (our complete family) were together traveling. I had shown an interest in fortune tellers as we traveled. My daughter, in the dream, tried steering me away from them; but I was persistent, saying, "I've got to go NORTH, I've got to go NORTH."

When she awoke, she knew the dream was telling her to pray for me; and that I was under heavy spiritual attack. North, she had researched, means spiritual warfare. When she called and began sharing, I started to cry. The dream had been sent to her in love- to join forces in being my prayer warrior. I was so blessed - but why? Why do we feel ever so blessed when we hear someone has had a dream about us and that they are shown to pray? I believe it is because we are reminded of how special we are to Him- that He is perfectly aware of our pain- that He is on our side, and will bring others to fight for us as well. I will be forever grateful to Jesus for this dream my daughter had; for it served as my lifeline for that day and in days to come.

HE SAID THAT SHE SAID

(May 13, 2012)

—⟨⟨∿⟩⟩—

Seems all my life I have struggled with gossip; first in my younger years now in my middle years. It is almost like a feeling of— better than— or superiority or worse still, something spicey and interesting to talk about- like what else is there to talk about?

This year I have made a more concentrated and deliberate effort to curb this sinful habit. I actually rinsed my mouth with salt water, repented, and invited the Holy Spirit to help me. I have slipped a lot since then, but feel I am making headway slowly, very slowly, but it is headway. Like any kind of addiction, it takes perseverance, determination and hatred of the habit. Most importantly, it takes help from Jesus. I have loved the clean feeling when I have 'passed' a particularly difficult gossip temptation. I am learning there are so many interesting ideas and things to talk about other than about cutting people down.

When I fail, Jesus tells me, "Get up, keep trying, until I can rise above all of this and win."

"Gossips can't keep secrets, so never confide in blabbermouths." Prov. 20:19 The Message Bible

THE BIG SISTER
(May 23, 2012)

—•%%•—

This is interesting dynamics; for initially the little sis learns by watching her big sis do life- like how she deals with stress, communicates with clerks, walks in integrity, and most importantly of all, how she sees, loves and worships her Lord.

But sometimes that little sister syndrome moves in reverse and the little sister can take the reigns. Then the big sis simply goes along for the ride—and it's all good because big sisters need breaks from their position at the bow of the ship and be able to sit back in the lounge chair of life and watch the fish swim by.

Big sisters need little sisters. Little sisters need big sisters. And so it is healthy, and so it is good.

ALL THE T'S CROSSED
ALL THE I'S DOTTED
'MOM, THEY'RE OUT OF BREAD
AND SOUP'
(May 31, 2012)

———<small>ℳ</small>———

It was May 31st- my daughter had called, frustrated about how her afternoon had gone- even calling it 'spiritual warfare.' It had started out an exciting day. She and her 9 year old daughter were on a special mother/daughter sleepover; one of their stops was to enjoy supper at the General Store Café; but the Café had run out of bread and soup. She had called me for suggestions on an alternative restaurant. I remember saying to her, 'Jess, there's a reason for this.' Earlier that day, I had listened to what proved to be a very important message from her—but her phone had not properly transferred it- so when I'd listened to it, there were barely any sounds. I had previously planned for them to stay in my 'wicker room/guest room' the following night. She loves that room. I had made a mental note on how to bless them. I was planning to purchase a plant for my daughter and pierced earrings for my granddaughter. Now she, assuming I had listened to her message, was merely calling to get some restaurant ideas before they arrive at my home. Of course I was then alerted to the fact that they were coming 24 hours earlier than preciously planned—(in 1 hour!) I quickly gave them a few suggestions and flew off on my errands. No sooner had I completed the final touches that they arrived at my home. As I was talking with her, I suddenly realized: Jesus had shown to me the "reason" for the restaurant disappointment- because had the first restaurant not been out of bread and soup and had she not called me to ask about a restaurant, I would not have been alerted to their 24 hour change of plans and would not have been able to bless them with my surprise gifts. Thank you Jesus—You are so into our daily details.

WHEN GOD CHANGES
THE WEATHER
(June 16, 2012)

—◦◦◦—

I had planned this event weeks ago. The Lord had blessed me in having me find this awesome affordable party barge. I had e-mailed family members and invited them for June 16th- in celebration of Father's Day. It was to be a surprise for my husband, Greg. That week I had found out the forecast called for 60% chance of rain. I was somewhat discouraged but announced: "I am going to pray for a sunny day." So my daughter and I started praying; and as each day grew closer to the event, I became more earnest. Early in the morning of the day, I ran to the window. The sun was peeping out- I began praising Him. Then two small showers came; I continued to believe He would answer my prayers. By 12:00 noon, the sun shone brightly. When we arrived at the dock on Medicine Lake, it was gorgeous and sunny. Our captain of the pontoon assumed we were not coming due to the forecast- so was shocked when I'd called saying we were at the dock waiting for him. He said, "You got lucky"—to which I answered, ' Luck had nothing to do with this , I prayed!' I later learned that there had been rain in other parts of town- but not on our Medicine Lake. The next day, it rained and rained. Thank you Jesus for hearing my prayers. You are so awesome!

FORGIVENESS AND THE ROBE OF RIGHTEOUSNESS

(June 23, 2012)

———✦———

What is it about forgiveness? I come to the table of forgiveness and I hear the promise of redemption; and I walk away, still clothed in sin and blackness? My head knows that is why Jesus died- so I can be forgiven and cleansed. Still each time I sin, I spend meaningless days continuing to beat myself up, wearing this shroud of guilt, reliving my sin act and thus re-nailing my Jesus to the cross. I want so much to know the feeling of fresh air and renewal- why does it take so long for my heart to receive? I am the great punisher of myself.

A DAY AT WALMART
June 22, 2012

———ɷɷɷ———

I stood in line- watching. She was spirited, warm and joy-filled. I was next and I heard her ask, "What's on the back of your shirt?" I turned around 'Got Fight' is what it read. She smiled and said she liked the shirt and the Bible verse: Psalm 118:17. I had worn it in preparation for my daughter in law, Judy's, picnic that day in celebration of her healing from breast cancer. The clerk added that she liked it that I too loved the Lord. She smiled and said she just wants to have others see Him in her. I told her I knew she loved Jesus when I was waiting in line. I then took her arm and told her to continue shining her light for Jesus. I added 'Never allow the world to squash you!' She smiled and under her breath, continued praising the Lord. I walked away with a song in my heart.

"Gracious speech is like clover honey. Good taste to the soul, quick energy for the body." Proverbs 16:24 The Message Bible

NUTS, GREEN APPLES, DISH SOAP

(June 24, 2012)

—◊◊◊—

I stop for a moment and gaze at my husband's shopping list. I cannot help but think of my list- the list that I have for Jesus- and all the lists of the world. I wonder what list is longer - the thank you ones or the 'I wants.' I sadly know what it is for me. Lord help me extend my thank you list and trust You more with my 'grocery list.'

OPEN OUR WINDOWS—SO WE CAN SEE—SO WE CAN HEAR
(June 27, 2012)

———

Today I walk to my bedroom window and see a friendly Robin perched on my roof's edge. It sings its lovely song. But I can barely hear him (the downside of air-conditioning). I miss God's nature songs. My Robin's song is muffled. Sometimes we only hear and see God's gifts in muffled tones- Let us fling open the windows and really see all that He gives to us with each new day!

WHEN GOD ORCHESTRATES OUR DAYS HE ORDERS OUR STEPS
(Sat. July 14 2012)

—◦◦◦—

I am amazed at how, if we stray from the best path, He re-positions the plan- because He loves us that much. Let me explain:

I had been counting the weeks- then the days- for my sister and niece to visit. Guthrie tickets had been purchased, house cleaned, fun places planned. Then the day before, I get the dreaded call: they cannot come. I remember saying, 'I feel so sad right now.' After a lengthy rescheduling, we ended the call. But as I walked around the house, I began to see that God was in this and that this was not the weekend for them to be here. I saw how that evening was set aside for a very important talk between my husband and myself. Jesus is all about communication. Jesus told me He could have had them come. He could have had it work out - but He'd stopped it for a reason. That evening, as my husband and I talked, I told him how I felt strongly that my niece and sister were not supposed to come this week-end; and that I believe we will even see more reasons why- as this weekend opens up. The next day, our daughter got sick- (which would have made it difficult to entertain her cousin). Then early the next morning, Saturday, my older daughter had come to our home, struggling and in need of prayer. This would not have been possible with a house full of company.

Next time, when plans get tumbled upside down and despair and discouragement follow- think of how God sees the picture; and since He wants the best for us- maybe He is simply re-directing, just tweaking our plans for our good.

HE CARES ABOUT EVERY ASPECT OF OUR LIFE-EVEN WHAT KIND OF CAR WE DRIVE

―――✺―――

After saving for many months, the time had come for me to purchase a different vehicle. I could not wait. But I soon became discouraged when I discovered the cars I liked were way out of my price range. We wrestled with taking out a larger car loan (which would take me about 2–3 years to pay off)- but did I really want to do that? Doors seemed to close one after another. I continued to pray. Then when I awoke one morning, I heard the Lord say, "Check your computer again downstairs." As I did, I came across a brand new entry on Craig's list—a black Ford Escape Limited 2005 $11,985.00-mileage: 77,469. I remembered back to a few weeks ago, when I thought I'd heard Him say, "You will own a black Escape." The ad fit all my qualifications - all! Then I googled what the difference is between an

Escape XLT and LT and Limited. The answer popped up: "top of the line." I sat there- tears flowing- as I thought how He loves to bless His children in extravagant ways: "top of the line." It was so Him. I quickly found out it was still available;—then called my husband. To my delight, he'd agreed to stop home and drive me over to look at it.

As I waited, I tried to get back on their site- but could not. When I tried to pull up the picture again, all I got was a blank. Hmmmm. Then the Lord spoke again. "He will take your bid." Hmmmmm . what bid? He also told me to praise Him for my new car. I thought, okay Lord, I will thank You for the car that I have not even seen yet.

When we arrived, I was nervous. The salesman took us to it. I loved it immediately and was once again awed by another one of my Lord's finger prints. The interior - only the Lord knew how much I loved light colored interior—a beautiful light-colored tan. We then took it for a spin, and threw in a bid. They told us that the bid was ridiculously low. We re-bid and waited. Then the manager sat down with us. He chopped off $1,113.75 and wrote the number $10,871.25. Okay- I had saved $9,000.00. I felt I could handle the difference with a small loan at my bank. As I look back at everything, I can see how all these details seamlessly unfolded by Your hands. You are awesome, Jesus- showing me how much You care-even about a little black 2005 Ford Escape.

PARENTS ARE:

—❦—

T he keepers of traditions—
Be heritage passers—
I, as the Matriarch, now have become the receiver of past traditions and will someday pass the baton so we can keep these precious ways alive.

A TRIBUTE TO MY DAUGHTERS

——⟨∿∿⟩——

They set the world 'in motion'.

They paint a day with bright fluorescent pinks, yellows and scarlet.

They walk into a room- and the brightest wattage unknown to man glistens in joyful grandeur.

Their words, well chosen, always seem to heal, love, soothe, touch, and cause a trembling heart to rest in calm repose.

They are an open vessel and God has poured out, through them, many parts of Him to this hurting world. Yet they remember to get replenished because serving Him is their delight.

They feel deeply, care openly, love unswervingly, and sacrifice quietly.

They carry many titles, yet refuse to wear any badge. Forerunners tend to do their work without fanfare or flags, yet the trail they leave behind them invites others to come and follow.

They are my daughters; truly women after the very core of the heart of my Lord! And I love them more than I can say!

ABOUT MY SALLY-MY BEST FRIEND

I remember quite vividly the first time I saw her. Being the "new kids on the block", (her husband was to be our new pastor at our church), she and her family were called to the front of the church for their blessing on his installation Sunday. I remember the dress she wore and although she walked up with her two children, I thought she looked like a little girl. It took me quite awhile to introduce myself to this lovely young woman. In time, I finally got up the courage. I remember apologizing because I had so rudely taken so long to welcome her. Being the person she is, she graciously thanked me and reassured me that now it would be easier for her to remember me because I didn't come clustered in with all the other women who had dutifully welcomed her in. As I look back on this memory, I'm amazed that we were younger then than our daughters are now!

MY DEAREST FRIEND, SALLY
(on her birthday party, Sept. 29, 2012)

———〜〜〜———

As you know, I am passionate about never taking one moment of life for granted. I stop to smell the roses and remind people to share their hearts with those they love, to never keep love hidden within. I also realize that I can fall into the trap of taking those endearing people in my life for granted, which is a strange and unreliable concept—that those we love will always and forever "be there". So today I want you to know how loved you are. The following is my way of telling you.

I have always looked at you as this rose, climbing and entwining itself among the thorns, passing through weeds, and breaking free from burrs and rubble. Though the rose passes in and amongst the garden's harshness, it remains as beautiful and sweet smelling as the day it blossomed. Though the world has tried its hardest to squash your delicate petals, you have risen and been a valiant warrior. Your beauty is glorious indeed!

"Friends love through all kinds of weather, and families stick together in all kinds of trouble." Prov. 17:17 The Message Bible

MOTHER'S TEA

(May 10,11th 2012)

—∿∿—

A warm welcome to all you beautiful mothers. The children and I have been quite excited to celebrate you today. We have planned sweet surprises for you. Now, please allow me a few moments of sharing from my heart.

It has been said that 'Motherhood is a partnership with God.' I so believe this for it is in this title known as 'mom' that we find ourselves most needy, most vulnerable, and most reliant on Jesus. We realize sooner or later that we cannot, or ever will, be able to do this job without our hands locked in His. And it is in this place of need, that a lovely friendship emerges; and we await His promised masterpiece: 'MOMS.' I liken parenting to that of painting a picture. Sure, you may attempt to take the brush and on your own create some design, but if you invite Jesus to place His hand over yours you will see His masterwork before your eyes. It is a beautiful sight to see our Lord's brush strokes on our children; for once you begin to see this, even if it is only in glimpses, you know that you are successfully passing on the baton.

Remember to memorize certain moments with your children, remain free to laugh, keep it real, and don't put off apologizing. More parenting is caught than taught—they are watching you watch Him, so pick up your brush. Can you feel His hand? What creativity, what a creation. You have now become a team and it shows.

I love you all,

Dee

THE DEDICATION OF
OUR SWEET CODY BROWN
(May, 6, 2012)

—◦◦◦—

"But Jesus said, "Let the little children come to Me, and do not forbid them; for of such is the kingdom of heaven" (Matt. 19:14 NKJV).

Cody- it is my prayer that you will grow in the knowledge of who this Jesus is that wanted all the children to come to Him. I pray you will come to know Him heart to heart—Your soul knowing Him like a brother, a father, a best friend and confidant. May you hear His voice, steering you in the direction He has planned for your life—and that nothing can stop you from pursuing that calling.

Cody- sweet Cody—Grandma loves you and wants you to know that nothing in the world can compare to knowing Jesus- I bless you with wisdom far above your years, and a joy that tickles heaven—may you have compassion for those less fortunate and a sensitivity to be able to touch the hearts of others in fresh new ways. May your path be hilly enough that you never ever lose sight of your need for Him. I pray you will come to know Him heart to heart—Your soul knowing Him like a brother and confidant. May you hear His voice, steering you in the direction He has planned for your life—and that nothing can stop you from pursuing that calling.

Cody- grow in Jesus and feel the breath of heaven on the pathway of your life's journey.

I love you,

Grandma

THOSE ELEVATOR PEOPLE AND OTHER ONE-TIMERS
(Aug. 2012)

———≈———

I walked into the elevator and quickly surveyed who was there: an elderly couple and a man in his 50's. Within seconds, the well-dressed elderly gentleman turned to me and said matter of factly, "It's the four of us." To which I responded, 'Yep. On a lovely Sunday morning.' His precious wife, by his side, answered emphatically, "Yes, it is." He then asked where I was from. After I'd answered, I returned the question. He answered just before the elevator's doors opened and they stepped out- not forgetting to tell me to have a good day. I watched as he most lovingly and gently ushered his wife down the hall to their hotel room, the younger man following. I turned to him and said, 'What a precious couple.' He said they were 96 years old and that he was their son-in-law. He agreed they were special. Then we parted ways.

But I began to think about all those elevator people—and waitresses and clerks and people we greet but once in our life and never see again. And I think are warmth and friendliness worth it? They are passing through - they are merely passing through our lives, like sand through our fingers. I think of the power in words and how just a quick smile could make someone's day. Yes, a kind word, or a simple thank you for services rendered—even for holding the door open. It's worth it- because they are creations of the King and love and a kind word will never ever return void.

"His Word will never return to Him void." (Isaiah 55:11)

THIS PLACE I AM IN

(Thurs. Sept 20, 2012)

—⟨∞⟩—

I remember parts of the prophecy, "You are like a butterfly to The Lord. You are moving into a new place." This precious man, likened to a prophet, had called me out of my staleness and I have since continued to step out of boat after boat- feeling His hands holding me up. So, what is this place and how have I changed? Well, for one, I am bolder - much more real with myself and people. I am transparent and less leaving things to guess and assuming— now I simply speak it out. Then there is the courage. I feel more equipped- like the Lord has brought me more tools to get the job done. I hear His voice speaking to my heart- sometimes clearly- sometimes not so clearly, still at peace knowing that I am surrounded by His heavenly hosts.

I love this place; and I will continue to seek Your face and hold Your hand as I continue my life's journey, ever so reveling in this place I am in!

"Sing to Him a new song. Play skillfully with a shout of joy, for the word of the Lord is right, and all His work is done in truth. He loves righteousness and justice; the earth is full of the goodness of the Lord." (Ps. 33:3 NKJV).

PAPPY'S POPPIES

(Oct. 3, 2012)

—◦◦◦—

I cannot recall when I began this - perhaps when my own mom was called home to be with Jesus. Whatever the reason, I have tried to stay on target for years now. Let me explain: every birthday of a loved one's who was close to my heart (whose residence now is 'heaven,') I send a personalized bouquet of flowers to them. For example, I know my mom loved Geraniums- bright orange- red ones. So, on her birthday, I like to send those to her. On my mother-in-law's birthday, I always like to send her a bouquet of pink flowers. (her favorite color was pink). I picture who is delivering them. Is it Jesus? So on this birthday, I decided to send something quite different to my mother. I asked Jesus to send her 3 dozen poppies (just like the ones my grandpa, I called him Pappy, had planted around the farmhouse so many years ago.) Happy Birthday mom! I love you!

THE BRIEFEST GLANCE

(Oct. 16, 2012)

—∿—

Sometimes, when I feel the Lord has granted me favor, grace, or a personal blessing, I will do a super quickie look upward to heaven. It's just my way of saying thank you. No one really notices. It's a little secret with my Jesus.

THE RECONCILIATION AN APPOINTED TIME EMPOWERMENT

(Nov. 8, 2012)

We had planned to attend a special dinner at the church where I teach. We had invited our son, daughter-in-law, and the 3 buddies. That afternoon, Jesus had assured me it would be lots of fun. But I felt anxious. I had previously been told that an old friend, a friend who had broken my heart, would be in attendance. As we all sat at our table- completely decked in white linen, enjoying one another, I asked my husband if he had seen them. He replied, "Why Yes, they are sitting right over there." I knew what I must do; and Jesus gave to me an empowerment to do it. So I turned to my daughter-in-law and said, 'I'm going to do it. I'm going to go pour hot coals.' Then I walked right over to her and gave her a huge hug. We clicked instantly; she received me, embraced me and we did a 15 minute catch-up. I met her 2 granddaughters and daughter-in-law. Then

I brought her to my table and introduced her to the buddies, Faith (my youngest daughter), my daughter-in-law and my husband; then she returned to her table. I felt this warmth, glow and peace begin to flood my soul and I knew I had been a part of something eternal- I had been obedient. I had experienced and walked into an appointed time! "For if you forgive men their trespasses, your heavenly Father will also forgive you. But if you do not forgive men their trespasses, neither will your Father forgive your trespasses." (Matt. 6:14–15 NKJV)

'I WANT MY PICTURE TO LOOK LIKE HIS'

(Dec. 31ˢᵗ, 2012—bringing in the New Year)

A s a pre-school teacher, I occasionally find myself sitting down with my children and coloring. Sometimes a child will study my picture and begin copying what I am drawing - same picture - same colors.

That, to me, is what I want to do with Jesus. I want my life's picture to 'look like His.' With His help, I want to use His same colors. He is my model. I am the copy-cat; and that is how it will be until I meet Him face to face. Jesus, I WANT MY PICTURE TO LOOK LIKE YOURS!

FOOTPRINTS IN THE SNOW

(Jan. 4, 2013)

The other day, my youngest daughter, Faith, and I were talking about all the footprints and animal tracks found in the snow. She'd mentioned that in winter, we get to see the animal tracking of every creature that has crossed our yard and their trail they took around and through. In winter, no tracks are hidden.

I like to think of our lives like that as well. Everything we do and say is never hidden from Him. Each life leaving tracks in the snow for our Lord to see. Lord, may my tracks be pleasing in Your eyes.

THOUGHTS ON WINTER
(March 24, 2013)

———

Oh winter will you ever run out of breath? Today is Faith's Gotcha Day. I remember well the day we flew out- March 24, 1996——a snowstorm here—raging in full force, as we headed to the airport. Now, today, 17 years later, flurries of snow blanket the land. I am homesick for summer and the greens and warm tan-colored skin, bare toes and sunshine that just won't quit. Come spring and once more cheer me with your presence.

THE DREAM
(May 2013)

—◦◦◦—

I had this dream. My daughter, Faith, and I were upstairs in the farmhouse where I was raised. A scary man was outside and yelling to us. "I'm coming up there to get you!" Faith immediately ran down the stairs and out the door. I then yelled to her: "Run Faith, run!" She safely got away. But then I heard him coming up the stairs to get me. I quickly opened up a window and jumped out all the way to the ground, and began running. Strangely, I kept thinking I had forgotten to put on my underwear that day. I was fully clothed- but just didn't have on underwear. So, I began running away. I ran until I came to a flea market. I ran up to the closest booth and told them a man was chasing me. She had a kind face but told me she could not help me. She then handed me a gift bag. I felt sad that she could not have helped, but kept running until I saw a bus. I got on and asked the people sitting across from me if they could help. They said they could not help either. I then asked the driver how soon until the bus would be stopping. He said 2 hours. I then told him I needed it to stop, 'Now!' He emphatically replied, "No!" He then heard me tell the people near me the story and became compassionate to me. He handed me a gift box and a ticket. He then said I was to cross the street, go into a building, down the steps, and I would be fine. So he stopped the bus. I did just as he had said. When I arrived downstairs, I discovered I was at my pre-school job with all the teachers I currently work with. They asked if I was okay. I proceeded to tell them what had happened. End of dream.

INTERPRETATION

—⁂—

I believe the farmhouse represents childhood generation stuff. The scary man after me represents generational fears, anxieties, and feelings of inferiority. The fact that daughter Faith escaped says to me that she has not been affected by my fears and generationally negative baggage. My escaping and running from the man is good- representing my own freedom and healing from these childhood scars. The fact of no underwear represents my own feelings of inadequacies and holding back- due to fears of being laughed at, teased, bullied and embarrassed. But I still manage to escape—meaning I am an over-comer. As For the people I met up with, (all fine and good) but unable to help me, I believe they represent the fact that people, though well meaning, are not going to be the ones to set me free—the Gift bag and the gift box I do not open to see what is inside. I am so pre-occupied to escape from the man, that I don't take time to see what is inside them. This, I believe, is KEY to my dream. I believe, tucked in those 2 gifts, are the "gifts" the "personal gifts" that Jesus has given to me that I have not used yet or have not utilized to the max. When I follow the instructions, crossing the street, entering the building and going downstairs, I am in my pre-school building. I believe that this is the place I am to be using the gifts that I have been given from Jesus. Okay, so what's in the box? What's in the bag? I believe one gift is the gift of the butterfly—letting go—not holding back—true personality—all my colors showing—for each feather has been placed there for a reason. What's in the other gift bag? I believe the Lord wants me to be bold, courageous and forthright- wake up, dust off, come alive, turn on my lights and shine them brightly!

THE PEACOCK STORY
(establishing my identity and walking in my destiny)
THE BIRTHDAY PARTY
(April, 2013)

—⟨⟨⟨⟩⟩⟩—

It was Beth's birthday party. Beth was my little student and the daughter of a dear friend of mine. My youngest daughter, Faith, and I had been invited. I believe Jesus had a message for me that day. I will tell you why.

It was a theme party—PRINCESSES!—Everyone was dressed up fancy; but more so was the way my friend's adult sisters were dressed and the magnetic charismatic personality of them. They permeated the party with their unique colorful styles. There they were in all their beauty, warmth, vivacity and passion. One sister wore high healed shoes, a party dress and done up hair - sparkling in personality, warmth and love. As I stood there fully enamored by their styles, I saw myself, shackled, behind bars of social embarrassment- like someone wearing too weird of a swimsuit and hesitant to come out of the water. Now, I see two women that were not afraid to show all their colors - no matter if they were different from the others or the world. I see many women as blah boring colors of browns and greys - non responsive, non feeling, no empathy. Blending in is their middle name; and so we take the safe, comfortable road offering a risk free carriage ride. We sacrifice lovely star light and sparkle because it's too awkward to stand out!

But that day became life-changing for me. It is like I now am able to see what I should be; and what that looks like. It begins with the prophecy over me. "A butterfly" free to be even if that means weird, emotional, empathetic, compassionate, dramatic, funny, or different. I am free to be me, all of me! There will be no boxes, no lines, no one to say act like this or act like that - be this or don't do that - don't be different - don't say that - fit in- keep your colors looking like the rest . .NO MORE . Let's consider the peacock——

He opens wide all his feathers - ALL his feathers; and Jesus wants us to open wide all our feathers. Some of those feathers may mean feeling different from the crowd, then so be it; for they are the colors that have been designed into us to bless the World. Lord, give me the courage to spread wide my colors so You can be glorified in each of them. Amen

THE SURPRISE BLESSING
(May 17th 2013)

—⟋⟋⟋—

It was Friday afternoon and my youngest daughter, Faith, and I decided to do some grocery shopping at our local Cub Food Store. As I placed the items on the belt, preparing to check out, I realized I had left my special Cub gas discount card and check card in the car. I quickly told the cashier I would be right back. Faith stayed back to watch the groceries. But when I'd returned to my car, I realized my wallet was not there. I had left it home. As fast as I could, I drove back to the house to look for it. I quickly grabbed it and raced back to the store. As I came running up to the cashier, there stood a lovely tall blond woman. She looked at me, smiled and said, "I paid for your groceries. I thought it would be a kind thing to do." My mind racing, and tears flowing, I hardly knew what to say. I gave her a big hug and said, "God bless you." She lovingly replied, "God bless you!"

As I drove home, recalling the event that just took place, I would tear up and a feeling of being loved on would wash over me. What are the thoughts that run through one's mind when one is blessed in such a generous way by a perfect stranger? We try to find reasons, explanations, and answers for it. You know, we humans have got to make sense out of everything. And I was no exception. My thoughts ran wild: 'It's Jesus blessing me for all the times I have blessed others' Or 'Jesus reminding me I am loved'. But as I think about it a bit more, I realize that it is not about me at all! It is about a woman who had listened to the still sweet voice of you, Jesus- and she took it and acted on it; and for a moment in time I felt bathed in the goodness of God. I felt Him smiling at me-overjoyed. There still remain those rare people in this world who find no greater pleasure than to simply bless others. I remain grateful to have been the one in the path of her generously loving gift.

PEACOCK STORY REVISITED
(May 19, 2013)

—∽∼∿∽—

I t was Sunday- and we were greeting at church. Then my dear friend and her family walked in and announced that she had had a dream about me. She then proceeded to share the dream: It was our Best Friend's Retreat. It was being held in a large home—not my house—but I was stressed over the house getting dirty and needing to be cleaned up, etc. I was powerfully ministering to women and making a difference. At that point, as she was sharing her dream, one of my friends from church walked over and began listening to the dream as well. She then took my hand and began ministering over me and interpreting the dream. She explained that God has given to me unique gifts and I was not to let the world take them away. She said I was to guard the ideals of my heart, which are the very things that make up the core of who I am. I am to guard against the world trying to squash them. I knew that a lot of it was in reference to my job as well—I cried because she was highlighting an area that Jesus knew I needed encouragement in. Later, after the service, another precious friend of mine, the husband of one of my friends, gave me a hug, looked at me and said, "Stay who you are." I knew it was confirmation of all that the Lord had been showing me since the 'Birthday Party.'

Dee, it is time, now, to get out those peacock feathers that I had stuffed in the drawer. You see, I only wore the safe and monotonous ones (the ones that don't stand out in a crowd). I had packed the unique and 'set apart' ones safely away. Well, it is clear to me that He wants those re-attached. He wants me to show my entire color palette to a world hungry for embellished brilliance——Lord, give me courage- freedom and confidence to walk in all that and more.

LOVE IS STRONGER STILL

(May 24, 2013)

—✍—

It was the morning of the last day of school. A precious mom was in my classroom sharing what turned out to be a 'life lesson' for me. She was telling me about her mother, whom I had befriended throughout the year. She said they had been talking about missing the school next fall (since her daughter had graduated). The grandmother had mentioned me. Because of a very painful past, the grandmother had given up on God and Christians altogether. She mentioned that I had shown her Love and tenderness that she apparently had not felt from other Christians. The mother went on to say that the grandmother said, "If this is what a true Christian is, then perhaps there is hope for me."

I am still in amazement- so it really is ALL ABOUT LOVE! Love really does cover over a multitude of sins. Yet still another reminder of why Jesus wants me to continue teaching. My ministry continues. Lord Jesus take my hand, give me counsel; and help me show this hurting world LOVE IS INDEED STRONGER STILL.

BEHIND THE
TRANSPARENT CURTAIN
(May 28, 2013)

—⁓—

This was interesting. I had chosen to teach the extra 2-week extended program at my pre-school. My class had a different crop of children. It had an unusual feel - some rude, some unruly, some compliant—yet distant. It had been a hard day. Then my husband spoke into the day in a way I had not seen. He mentioned that what I pour into my class shows on the outside; and these children had not been in my class this past year. I realize this comment can be interpreted as 'puffed up' or proud and bragging. But it is so not meant to be taken that way. I believe Jesus is telling me- encouraging me- that I DO make a difference in the lives of these children. What I present to them matters- that the love I have for Jesus spills out to them—that The gifts He has given to me that I pour into them shows. It is not invisible; for it is felt with the heart by parents and seen with the visible eye.

LISTEN——TO A CHORUS IN JUNE
(June 1, 2013)

———

The month of June—budding with a freshness all of its own. Early I walk to my garden to snap off some Lilies of the Valley for my daughter-in-law. As I gather these delicate white bells, I am reminded of the sounds so familiar to my ears—yet, at the same time brand new and bold to the soul - like the symphony of birds blending in easy harmony, then interrupted by the cooing of the doves, which isn't really an interruption at all- but instead purposely written into the script of summer. Suddenly, a comforting distant sound of a train awakens my senses. I am smiling now and loving this morning in June——when the chorale of heaven and the sounds of earth collide in a heavenly chorus in June.

GOD'S SYMPHONY THERE'S BEAUTY IN HIS SILENCE

(June 2, 2013)

—⁂—

I am taking mental notes on beauty all around—silently—ever so silently—the lilacs come, blooming fragrantly soft. How many times have I buried my face in their purple clusters? The bridal veil dotted with all of June's fresh paint, and the world begins to come alive. Our dear mother's ornamental crab apple trees, having given off their pink splendor, now stand green and simple- yet splendid and soft—swaying to the breezes in the balance of life. My flower bed pops with Columbine, Lilies of the Valley, and one bold Iris. The Peonies patently await their turn.

I look at Spring as God's Symphony—the Conductor positions Himself. Holding His baton, he orchestrates each set of instruments -when to come in, when to fade out. Then the piccolo, next the flutes—the violins and the drums for emphasis. Just as there is a time for each stringed instrument, so there is for the percussion,—offering their notes precisely. So it is with these gorgeous beauties. Each one takes its place—performing in the beauty of its blossoms. I don't want to miss any of the music! Lord Jesus, keep me alert, watchful and tuned to each new paint stroke of Yours, every new note. For it is the rhythm of Your song. It is the portrait of Your canvas. It is Your performance; and I am the audience. I clap . I smile. I become part of Your portrait, flowing and dancing to the beat of Your concert.

THE GREAT PLAN
(June 8, 2013)

—◊◊◊—

I believe that every one whom the Lord allows us to have a relationship with is for a unique and personal reason- meant to add a new dimension to our lives and enhance and better equip and sharpen the tools that already exist within us; in other words, we have something that we are to pass on to them, and they have something that they are to pass on to us. By doing so, we can then see THE GREAT PLAN—like observing an architect, as he meticulously sketches away- to produce the finished product. We are continuously in process of moving more and more into our destiny. Lord, help me move to the sketches of Your plan for me.

THE COLOR GRAY
(June, 2013)

—⁓—

I hate the color gray. To me, it is a color that replicates drab, dull, depressing, plain and boring. A gray day can drop my Spirits like none other; and no one really looks good in gray. It turns a complexion from rosy pink to sullen ashen and ages women immediately.

It seems there is an overabundance of 'gray people' passing by- that appear to not care about others. You can spot them by The 'color' they give off-you guessed it- gray——that expres-Sionless face, all of them walking to the same gray beat. Jesus, give me courage to SHINE with my favorite color: NEON PINK! Even when it hurts, even when I'm slapped down, even when I feel I am the only neon pink person left on the planet. Help me radiate YOU, because just maybe if I plant enough pink seeds, they perhaps may grow a garden of rainbow colors!

AND SO THE SYMPHONY CONTINUES GLIMPSES OF HEAVEN
(June 20, 2013)

—*∞*—

The Iris have quieted as the Peonies take center stage- The softest pinks and the boldest fuchsia meet head on in all their splendor. The subtle Columbine settle for background beauty- yet remain playing their gentle tune. I see the Clematis in the wing, waiting for its cue from its Heavenly Creator; and all this is enhanced by the songs of bird calls. Every now and then a Whippoorwill chimes in- and the cooing of the dove seems to complete spring's aroma. A gentle breeze brushes over me, am I in heaven? No, but He has given to me glimpses, a sort of 'tease' of what is to come. I am enamored by the beauty- like I am experiencing it all for the very first time. I continue to drink from God's summer fountain; and like a cold glass of pink lemonade on a hot summer's day, my soul is quenched by its magic.

"Many oh Lord my God, are Your wonderful works which You have done" (Psalm 405A NKJV).

MY SEASON FOR COMING INTO
(June 20, 2013)

———∾∾∾———

Today my spirit seems intensely heightened and keenly aware of life around me- like things make sense, seem clearer and I feel loved. I feel a purpose to my life and a firmness in my step- like I am in sync with my Creator-stepping to the beat of my rhythmical destiny. I feel I have something to say; and people are listening. I believe my words do not fall on deaf ears. I am seeing the plan- like a curtain that suddenly becomes transparent. I am dreaming- do not wake me from my reverie of bliss. Oh let me not wander from this beautiful place I am in. Yes, I am in a season of coming into my own.—I have always been a late bloomer; some things never do change, do they? "Behold I will do a new thing. Now it shall spring forth, shall you not know it? I will even make a way in the wilderness, and rivers in the desert." (Isa. 43:19 NKJV)

SEQUEL TO MY SYMPHONY
(Aug. 11, 2013)

Gently, softly-spoken—small purply flowerlets can be heard- dotting my garden- reminding me that the season of flower color is drawing to an end. I sit and listen to the last few stanzas known as summer.

THE WALKING ZOMBIES
(June, 2012)

—⟡—

D id you ever notice the blah, grayish feel in stores these days? It is almost like there is a perpetual cloudy-day feel throughout public places. It is not just among the clerks, but the customers as well——people all walking around with glassy-eyed dullness and robotic gestures -saying as few words as possible, even then unfeeling and monotone; and it is rampant. It is everywhere!

But, like a small delicate violet in a bed of rocks, every so often you meet a person who lights up the surroundings like the 4th or July fireworks in a dark summer's sky. The vivacious personality ignites her dull surroundings and she envelops us with her sunshine; and the day suddenly turns sunny! Oh you see them placed here and there, chatting with the customers or clerks—like bright beams of lights-almost like a shake-up to the sleeping souls. Lord, give me the courage to be that ray of light—to rattle the cages of mediocrity and mundane and to scream to the world; 'WAKE UP, SMELL THE FLOWERS, SMILE, COME ALIVE, BE KIND, AND SPREAD GOD'S JOY AND LOVE TO A WORLD SO VOID OF HIM!'

AN ANGEL NAMED CAROLINE

—∞—

I met her for the first time in a small town café in upstate Buffalo, New York. We were taking my husband's 87 year old father out for breakfast. He had spoken very well of her; and now we were going to meet her. I enjoyed watching the special relationship they shared. She carried a kind sort of confidence; and when he got this horrible coughing spell, she walked by our booth and intentionally replied, "Arms over your head, Cal." I later learned she and her family had included him at their 4th of July festivities- along with a trip to the airport when he was visiting his sister.

Caroline is not a family member, nor a neighbor; but as I watched her in action, I realized that this is what loving in the real world is all about. Caroline does not have an impressive long title. She does not inhabit an office with a brass plated name on the door. She does not have notoriety for being this or that. But in the eyes of my husband's dad, she is 'Jesus with skin on'; and I feel ever so privileged to have met her.

"Then the King will say to those on His right, 'Come, you who are blessed by my Father; take your inheritance, the kingdom prepared for you since the creation of the world. For I was hungry and you gave me something to eat, I was thirsty and you gave me something to drink, I was a stranger and you invited me in, I needed clothes and you clothed me, I was sick and you looked after me, I was in prison and you came to visit me.' "Then the righteous will answer him, 'Lord, when did we see you hungry and feed you, or thirsty and give you something to drink? When did we see you a stranger and invite you in, or needing clothes and clothe you? When did we see you sick or in prison and go to visit you? The King will reply, 'I tell you the truth, whatever you did for one of the least of these brothers of mine, you did for me.' (Matt. 25:34–40 NKJV)

THE HIGH SCHOOL REUNION

(August 10, 2013)

A perfect example of time passages is a high school reunion. They are all talking about their jobs, how many children they have, some are expecting; and life is new and the world is ripe for adventure—new exploits to unfold. Decades later, we once again attended my husband's reunion. This time it was very different.

A sparse few stood off in a corner talking of their jobs, but most have long since retired. Now it is how many GRANDCHILDREN do you have? Some have left their spacious four bedroom homes and have moved into retirement communities. Many of the men are balding or totally bald, grey or white—and actually have an elderly aura about them. Some of the women suffer from rheumatoid arthritis- and there is a list on the back table of all the fellow classmates that are now deceased. It reminds me of a classroom spelling bee—who will be 'left standing' and who will have to 'sit down'—

As I look into their now senior faces, I try to turn back the clock and imagine what all of these people looked like 46 years ago————their wrinkles gone and all facial structure secure, in tact and distinct- eyes bright and ready to take on the world. They stand erect with white teeth and a youthful twinkle in their eyes. How high can I jump? How far can I run? How fast can I drive? Where is the best place to grab a pizza? Where did you get those darling boots?

But I am quickly brought back to the present. She is talking to me about her 40 pound weight loss, her arthritis, her recent retirement and how many grandchildren did you say you have? And so I listen. I hear a different song now; but there is still a sizzling. She is content; she is peaceful and her eyes speak of hope; and though we are all here for the same reason - to celebrate where we have been, we also celebrate where we are going. There is much more to come - life is full of more to discover, more to unfold; and I feel a surge of gratitude for where I am at.

The Master of Ceremony suddenly announces there is a band and dancing music upstairs. We decide to join them. My husband requests, 'Unchained Melody' and a bunch of couples enter the dance floor together. We are no exception. It is fun; and as we dance, I know that as long as I feel '16,' I will never grow old.

So high school reunions come and high school reunions go - but as long as the spirit soars, as long as there is a dance floor and music to dance by, I will remain undaunted by age—I feel young and therefore I am.

GONE TO THE WIND

(August 13, 2013)

—⁘—

D id you ever have one of those times when it felt like a handful of friends are gone to the wind? Allow me to explain. I know that everyone has their own scenario- but for me, it begins with a thought—"But she said she was going to Give me a call next week. Now it is going on the third week?" Or you call a friend and somewhere in the middle of the conversation, they suddenly have to 'run'—but say they will call you 'right back' in 10 minutes. Those 10 minutes never do come. In the same week, I think about an old friend that I have not seen in months. I become curiously consumed—so I venture the call. We talk for 5 minutes and then, in the middle of my sentence, I hear—'Dee, Dee, Dee, Dee, I have got to go, I am late already.' So I wait a few days and decide to call a few more friends- no one is home so I leave messages.

Oh I realize and understand, but when all this happens in the same week, my brain plays tricks, and subconsciously categorizes the week: Friends - Gone With the Wind.

MY ADDRESS BOOK
(Aug 28, 2013)

In my lifetime, there is something very priceless and irreplaceable to me: my address book. It is old now, the binding ripped and shredded. I have gone through it several times, adding this, erasing that; and it is this crossing out and erasing that gets me thinking and causes me to pause. Just how many names have I erased from the pages of this book in the span of 40 years? I really don't want to know. First, it began with a name here and there, to erase or cross out, those that had passed on. Then perhaps a change of address of some who have moved far away and sadness sweeps over me like a dark shadow and I am reminded of how delicately awesome life is. It is a travesty to take any one for granted. Life's greatest gifts are the people we love and cherish each and every day of our lives.

My address book is old and a continual reminder to me that we are all pilgrims only passing through.

POP
(July, 2013)

—∿∿—

I love the word: 'POP'

This is an onomatopoeia word—and works for just about everything. Colors 'pop' and can turn a room 'on'! Clothes 'pop,' hair styles 'pop' and even certain hair colors can 'pop'! But there is one thing that's my favorite: 'PEOPLE POP'! Unfortunately, most people don't . But those that do, they actually can explode with life; and I want to hang all around them, hoping that some of their glitter will rub off on me. It's like I cannot get enough of them.

WHEN LOVE WRITES
(my birthday, July 10, 2013)

—◈—

Sometimes a love letter becomes more than just a love letter. It seems to come to life; and visual imagery so keenly written that one cannot separate the penned prose from the heart's emotions. Sometimes love letters can be so inspired that one stands in awe of just such a masterpiece. These letters overflowing with love, are metaphorically profound and wonderfully lovely.

Sometimes a love letter IS the gift. (in reference to the beautiful writings I receive from my husband)

Our recent trip to Paris—the Eiffel Tower-quite a masterpiece of architecture. September/October 2014

Tender moments—a lifetime of memories and counting

Greg with our two amazing sons: from left to right: Christopher and Josh.

Here we are with a handful of our awesome grandchildren—5 are missing from this picture.

NOT LONG ENOUGH THAT
ANNOYING AGENDA
(July 23rd, 2013)

———

Seems like most of the things I absolutely adore doing end way too early in their lifetime. I then feel like I am left holding the bag. It never fails, when I am embracing heaven in some super fun activity, there appears someone who looks at her (his) watch and announces they need to end this crystal moment because of their.(yep that's it) agenda. Agenda, agenda, agenda. If it is not agenda, it is time to sleep, time to rise, time to eat, or time to clean up. Time to, time to, time to. I would just love to be with someone who comes with an open, empty agenda jar; and time can drift by unnoticed as we get lost in the reverie of merely being together- heart- to- heart - sharing golden moments; and as time tiptoes by, it becomes almost invisible, finally losing its relentless momentum. 'Time to' stop knocking at my door and go away . I'm just not interested!

LONELINESS
(July 11, 2013)

———∿∿∿———

Loneliness is keeping busy; because it hurts so bad, and busy-ness numbs the pain.

Loneliness is turning the TV on- just to listen to a different voice other than the one inside of you that says you are worth nothing. Watching TV can drown out the deafening silence and silence can sometimes be your worst enemy.

Loneliness is watching a beautiful summer's sunset alone.

Loneliness is watering my lovely veranda flowers that rest by 2 chairs that also sit alone, wanting so much to sit beside someone I love, to talk to, dream, to say I love you, as the world walks by on the sidewalk in front of you.

Loneliness is looking at my lovely screened in porch- but seeing no one out there- just flowers and plants that hang pretty for me; but no one else to enjoy them.

Loneliness is feeling unloved, boring and out of step with this fast-paced, technology-drenched world.

Loneliness is me.

"I will lift up my eyes to the hills from whence comes my help? My help comes from the Lord, Who made heaven and earth." (Ps. 121:1 NKJV).

WHEN THE DUCKS ARE
ALL LINED UP

—⦿—

Isn't it interesting- just what defines: "When the ducks are all lined up"? It can be different with each individual; but to me it is 100% people related. It begins early in the day—and if it is a sunny warm day, that is even better. But it appears that the first action or (duck) begins the task of encouraging you. The next 'duck' then does the same (however that may look). I love those kind of days. I feel worthy, important, and glad to be here. Thank you Jesus for these days.

70 X 7

(Oct. 1, 2013)

———∿———

After an unusually painful and disturbing 3 weeks at work, I woke early one morning to a remarkable revelation: "70 X 7." After the pain has been inflicted and the dust has settled- and all the plans to retaliate have been laid aside, one thing still stands true: 70 X 7.

70 X 7. It is still the only way. Guarding my heart, He is making me stronger, building courage and muscles in me——all this is true and good. But, still, above all else . 70 X 7!

"At that point Peter got up the nerve to ask, "Master, how many times do I forgive a brother or sister who hurts me? Seven?" Jesus replied, "Seven! Hardly. Try seventy times seven." Matthew 18:22 The Message Bible

PENNIES IN THE SAWDUST
(Feb. 11, 2014)

—◈—

These are harsh weeks- winter- peaceful but oh so long. I feel closed up in a cave—so much darkness, so little light. We walk it out. I remember as a child, attending our church's yearly summer picnic. They would have a sawdust pile- and in it were hidden pennies. At the count of "go," we children would go to it, digging in the dust, trying our hardest to gather as many pennies as we could find.

I feel that is how I live in winter. I strive to plan as many fun times as I can throughout those cold dreary months- not unlike searching for the pennies. I close in on one, drop it in my pocket and over and over again the search continues. It's really just a coping style—and in the end I have collected a pocket full of winter memories.

WE PRACTICE PRESENCE
(March 2, 2014)

—⟨⟨⟩⟩—

I was visiting with a dear teacher- friend while doing my youngest daughter's High School conferences. Though my daughter had never had this particular teacher, our friendship has remained strong. She was excited to tell me of the newest love of her life: a brand new granddaughter; and another grandchild soon to arrive. I congratulated her and then added, 'if I send you an invite, would you come to our daughter's graduation open house?' She replied that she will if she is in town - that there would be showers and the baby is due in June. Then she proceeded to say something that really stayed with me, "We practice presence." I looked at her pensively and knew exactly what she meant. "You do it too," she added. Though I have never put a name to it, she was right. For PRESENCE IS EVERYTHING! It is stronger than anything, more powerful than words, beautifully calligraphied on expensive parchment paper. One's presence has that profound and extraordinary ability to push everything else aside and take front and center stage. Presence, one of the loudest ways to love.

TOUGH AS HIDE

(March 2, 2014)

—⟨⟨⟨⟩⟩⟩—

I hate being tough as hide. It is not me. I must strive to go into that room and pull on those boots. They fit me poorly and I feel in bondage. But I thought when one "lets things roll off one's back," and "not take on offenses, " you would feel set free. But I really don't at all. I, instead, feel plundered upon and injured. There is that microscopically fine hair-like line that we must see. I mean there are sometimes moments when one must say something- do something. I am told I have a gift of forgiveness. Could it be that some people can stomp and stretch on that until there is barely anything left? The term: 'boundaries' is the word of the 21st Century; everyone's boundaries look differently. I try my hardest to wear these boots- sometimes they fit tighter than at other times; but ultimately, freedom will always fit most comfortably. So whether I need to: 'clear the air' and 'talk it out,' or 'let it pass,' I do know that one's spirit needs to fly- however that may look to each one of us. If you can allow things to roll off, you are free. If you need to do a "we need to talk," then do that- but above all, try your hardest to remain in control.

WHEN HE HIDES SURPRISE PACKAGES TUCKED INTO OUR DAYS
(March 3, 2014)

—◦◦◦—

I had walked a painful weekend and began my Monday with tears and confusion. A few days earlier, I had made an appointment at a skin rejuvenation clinic and drove to it wishing I could just stay home. But upon entering this place, I was refreshed by the warm greeting- and delightful tray with green tea and nut snacks. As I filled out the necessary questionnaire, I suddenly noticed the song that was playing in the room, "I will rejoice, I will give praise, God is my victory and He is here!" I could not believe my ears—— Christian music playing in a secular place? As I was ushered to a room, I was introduced to a lovely woman named Cora. From the moment we began talking, we clicked. The love she showed me was refreshingly real. We talked of Christian events, Beth Moore, Joyce Meyers, Women of Faith and Day Set Apart for Women. I told her how much I was blessed by the peacefulness and Christian music. She thanked me and said she had had a rocky morning and so needed my encouragement. Just before leaving, I asked if I could pray for her. As I asked the Lord to bless her and her business, she began to cry. When I left, I felt my spirit rejuvenated. Just think, I came to have my face rejuvenated, and left with my spirits lifted. Jesus, You knew what I needed today- and I feel like I have been touched by Your love with a cherry on top. I returned home to listen to a phone message: The person had listened to my 'sorry we are not at home- God bless you' message and had added, "God bless you too." Today Jesus gave to me packages all wrapped up in His 'rejuvenating love'! Thank you Jesus—thank you.

WHEN GOD SPEAKS
(June 20, 2014)

———

A beautiful bird singing, a scampering squirrel on a soft summer's morning———but I felt like crying, as I shuffled around the house- doing this, doing that. I continued my prayer, 'Jesus, send me a hummingbird for my feeder. I want to see just one.' I had set it up a week earlier and had promptly filled it with the necessary sugar mixture. I needed a sign today of His personal love for me. Someone once told me that only weak Christians ask for 'signs.' Well, then I guess I am weak. Earlier this morning, I had read what Jesus had to say in my devotional, Jesus Calling for June 20th. I paraphrased it as follows: "I speak to you all day long. I love to talk with you., though not always in words. I fling glorious sunsets across the sky day after day after day. I caress you with a gentle breeze that refreshes and blesses you. I speak softly in the depths of your spirit, where I have taken up residence. You can find Me in each moment, when you have eyes that see and ears that hear. Ask my spirit to sharpen your spiritual eyesight and hearing. I rejoice each time you discover I Am with you. Practice looking and listening for Me during quiet intervals. Gradually, you will find Me in more and more of your Moments. "You will seek Me and find Me, when you seek Me above all else." Jeremiah 29:13. Then, as God would have it- I was passing through the dining room and happened to look out at the Hummingbird feeder, when I saw it—my Hummingbird busily feeding away. Tears filled my eyes as I dropped to the floor in gratitude; and I heard Him say, with a smile, "This was for you, My Dee." Oh how I needed His reassurance, oh how He had filled my cup!

SUMMER'S ENTRANCE
(June 21, 2014)

———⟨⟩———

Summer awakens life and the newborn bunny hops on my front sidewalk, nibbling tiny stray grass. A Hummingbird grabs a morning snack and I feel I have tasted a bite from heaven. The stillness of a summer's morning brings peace to my parched soul- and I can feel the breath of His love. A bird sings as if to echo my emotion. The earth comes to life and I as well!

THIS DAY

(July 4th, 2014)

—⟨∿⟩—

I am marveling at the beauteous perfection of this day. The symphony croons as I busy myself watering hanging baskets, and refilling the bird bath. The weather echoes God's love; and I inhale His glorious personal love for me, His Dee, His Own. The peacefulness of the morning brings me to a Holy place; and I am immersed in His presence. Sometimes Heaven does come down here, sharing with us pieces of what is just around the bend. Thank you, Jesus, for THIS DAY!

CRYSTAL GOBLETS AND
SILVER PLATTERS
2 Timothy 2: 20–21 (The Message Bible)

———

"In a well furnished kitchen, there are not only crystal goblets and silver platters, but waste cans and compost buckets—some containers used to serve fine meals, others to take out the garbage. Become the kind of container God can use to present any and every kind of gift to His guests for their blessing."

As I read this, for some reason, this stands out to me in bold letters- almost like it had been high-lighted! I sit here thinking about it and I think it is a message for me.

I want to be used by Jesus not only as I want myself used (in a more prestigious style- with fanfare and acknowledgement) the crystal goblet and silver platter kind of ministry——but Jesus wants me to be willing to be the container used to take out the garbage, if needed, as well. I need to be humble and aware, with a big enough vision to see that sometimes He may need to use me in a way that is not very flattering to the naked eye—like when I am asked to change a stinky diaper, listen to a rambling hurting heart, stay when I want to leave or cry with someone when I would prefer to laugh with another. Sometimes God calls us to be crystal goblets; and those are really fun moments. We are ministering, serving and also loving every minute - saying neat things like: "For this I was made"! But Lord, make me aware of the 'other times,' when it hurts so much to minister, to be used as the waste can or compost bucket. But if I know that it is YOU that placed me there, then I will serve You well no matter what the container, no matter what the use, for I am Yours and I serve in whatever the capacity You need me.

Lord, help us all to drink of the sweetest of wine, or the smelliest of compost for it is all the same to You.

PAIN, EXCRUCIATING, EVEN STILL, THE PROMISE

(August 19, 2014)

—◦◦◦—

When the pain swooshes over the heart like 20 foot waves, all one has is breath, though ever so slight, to whisper His name -"Jesus." When memories plant themselves in ever-widening circles around our spirits and the homesickness becomes almost unbearable, there is just one place to go- into His arms, where He reminds us to trust, wait, trust and see that His promises are real.

The words of trust that I write are not what I feel as of now. But I know enough to say that what my heart feels and what is fact fight each other. So though heaven looks awfully tempting today, I somehow know that my Jesus has got to be cooking up something awfully good. All this pain has got to be worth something. It has got to be worth something. So I hang on by threads, though microscopically in size and believe in a God that loves me way too much to let me drift much longer. But for now, I choose to trust- breathing, eating, talking, praying, crying and listening to His voice. "Weeping may endure for the night, but joy comes in the morning." (Ps. 30:5 NKJV).

LOOK AT THIS PICTURE

Look at this picture, and you will see
When we were together you and me.

We laughed and we cried
And I was right there
Right there by your side.

Through the thick,
Through the thin,
We've walked it together
Through the outs
Through the ins
And all kinds of weather.

Oh where have the years gone?
And whence did they fly?

And babies and loved ones
And pies in the sky?

We've memories, history
Carved by just us.

A quilt sewn and fashioned
From years smooth and years rough.

But study the quilt closely
And there you will find
It is truly unique-
A one of a kind.

For hidden within all the bright colors and prints
Is a patch so worn and faded
One can hardly depict.

That it has been there forever
From when it was first sewn
When the quilt was first stitched
So many years ago.

This patch has endured
Many washings and wear

And has a few rips and quite a few tears

But the patch has been sewn, holding the others together

For the patch is my love and my love is FOREVER!

H appy Anniversary to the love of my life! On our 45th anniversary

Your Forever Dee

ROSES ALONG THE WAY

(August 29, 2014)

———✍———

Have you ever looked back on a painful time in your life—and discovered that you had gathered roses precisely placed on the pathway in various places at opportune times? It is most difficult to realize they are roses or, for that matter, that they are even there while you are walking through it; but, later you see the pattern emerge and looking closer still, see His fingerprints on each petal.

Sometimes I can actually count and name precisely when each rose appeared. The first was a simple comment from my daughter—wrapped in hope and embraced in love. The second came via a text, reminding me that there are angels all around me. The third literally WERE roses! Yes, no need to go further there. The fourth came through an e-mail once more pouring hope into a parched heart. I think of His promise to us: "All you need to remember is that God will never let you down; He'll never let you be pushed past your limit; He'll always be there to help you come through it" (1 Cor. 10:13). Thank you for keeping Your Word, Sweet Jesus, thank you for keeping Your Word!

THE MICRO LASER PEEL

(August 27, 2014)

—⟨ᴓᴓ⟩—

It is day 3 of my infamous 'micro laser peel.' I say 'infamous' because it is costly and rather vain. But, I have saved for it, and feel grateful I am able to maybe subtract a few years from my face.

But as I was thinking about this procedure and its downtime etc., I could not help but see a lovely analogy emerging. And it could not have come at a more poignant time. Allow me to explain:

This procedure is not provided free. It comes with a cost (a stout cost) along with somewhat of a discomfort, massive redness, and swelling. Thick, rich ointment is then applied over the entire face and neck each day and night to keep it hydrated. Then there comes the peeling out the Kazoo! Now the peeling is very important. For it is in the peeling that the lovely new pink and healthy skin surfaces. And oh how fresh, clean and vibrant that is! But, remember, it comes only after the rough abrasive laser treatment—AFTER THE TREATMENT! I know you are already seeing the 'surface' here.

Throughout this time, I guess one could say, I have walked a 'procedure.' My heart has seen and has felt pain, abrasive pain; and the cooling ointments of friends have been both supportive and sustaining. But the true work, from the inside out, is what my Jesus does. Because what begins to surface, after healing has taken place, is more beautiful than words can describe. Deep, rich, costly understanding like none other - like being led into a room that you did not even know existed! And when you look around, you don't ever want to leave for its architecture was most dramatically built with you in mind, but with less of you and more of Him. I realize that is hard to grasp. Let me put it another way: when one feels overweight and loses those extra pounds, there is "less" of that person, yet "more" because now that person is healthier, more vibrant, and likes oneself more. It's basically a case of "less is more"!

So, life lessons (the hard kind), come with a price. And this ticketed price can never be afforded without His strength, down-loading, the tenderness of friends, and His 24/7 Presence. Thank you, Sweet Jesus, for keeping your Promises. You, my great Physician, are constantly taking care of my old skin cells, and rejuvenating new ones each step of my way to Eternity. I hope my skin will be rosy and bright when I some day see You FACE TO FACE!

WHEN TRAVELING THROUGH DEEP DARK FORESTS-THERE DOES COME THE PROMISED LIGHT

Sunday, August 31st, 2014.

—⟋⟋⟍—

I have walked, no, trudged on scary rocky cliff-like paths, that really weren't even 'paths' at all, except for the fact that Jesus had previously trudged them. I have hurt so painfully that I have taken sleeping pills so I could sleep the day away because there is no pain when I am asleep. I have refused food and drink and know the feeling of being disappointed in the morning, because I woke up.

In essence, this time has come with a great price. Doesn't anything that is worth anything come with some kind of price? This I am sure of:

To trust in Jesus is EVERYTHING! If I don't have that, I have nothing. I look back for a moment on the journey I have just trod and I shudder because a few times my foot did slip, some gravel beneath my feet fell thousands of feet below, but I did not fall. I know that I was held, maybe not sure footed, but I was held nonetheless.

Life lessons are rarely, if ever, learned easily. The price is costly: A bleeding heart, tears of anguish, homesickness, loneliness, and emptiness within plagued me constantly. Still, His presence (though not felt at times) was constant and His arms are long and strong. He had hand picked friends from His garden that stood by, watching, praying, calling, texting, being, holding, soothing. I have learned more than I can write in this letter, and yes, it was worth it.

Now as I continue this journey, I feel a bit more sure-footed and lightened by no more chains. Of one thing I am certain: I am loved, freely and unconditionally. I know that there is and always will be just one "me". I have a journey that is mine and my face is pointed ahead. I hear the cheers, I feel His push. I walk this marathon called life and will someday fall into His arms and know I finished well.

"I have fought the good fight, I have finished the race, I have kept the faith. Finally there is laid up for me the crown of righteousness, which the Lord, the righteous Judge will give to me on that day, and not to me only but also to all who have loved His appearing." (2 Tim. 4:7–8 NKJV).

My Dear Precious Son:

I think this is the year to present you with this. I so cherish it. Here is why:

In the fall of your 3rd year on the face of this earth, I bought you a little plastic clown costume. I could not wait to place it on you - oh you looked so cute in it. I then proceeded to decorate your face to complete the ensemble. We then headed out to various homes in our little South Minneapolis neighborhood. Your little self walking beside me and that little trusting hand holding mine was so endearing. We talked and we walked, we walked and we talked. I remember thinking that this is an awesome time in my life, almost spiritual, and feeling,(even before I knew the word) like this was rare and kyros in all respects. It was a feeling of time out of time, like this would be a "once in a lifetime" kind of moment.

I tucked that little costume away and it has lived in my hope chest for many years. It is the only costume I have ever saved! Now, my dear son, your own son is that age; and though he will probably never ever wear it (clowns are 'out' you know) I still want you to have it - and once in a while get it out, hold it, and know that there was a moment when you were little, we walked together, and life was ever so good.

I love you Brownerella!
Mom

ROSES AND REESE'S PIECES

—◦◦◦—

Some people have the most unique relationship with Jesus. But then again, if we (each one of us) take time to get to know Him, we will discover we also can have that personal relationship with this King of Kings. So here's our story:

Things were not going very well in the boy/girl relationship status with my youngest daughter and her boyfriend. She had waited long enough for things to change and had decided to invite him over and have 'the talk' with him. She was planning to put a closure on this 14 month relationship. It was a rough and tense day. As we plowed through our errands, I felt sad and ill at ease. I knew what was ahead for him, as well as for my daughter. She was dreading it but ready to get it over with. Suddenly the doorbell rang and I heard her say, "He's here." As she welcomed him in, I noticed she wasn't saying anything. I was perplexed and quite curious. I then noticed she was carrying roses and a bag of Reese's Pieces into the kitchen (but still not talking). "Mom, (she barely got the words out), could you please take care of these roses?" She and her boyfriend quickly left the room. They were upstairs for what seemed forever. When she came downstairs, she shared with me something that will forever be branded on my heart:

What I had not known is that before her boyfriend arrived, she had facetiously/sarcastically prayed to Jesus. It went something like this: " Okay, if I am not supposed to break up with Him, then have him bring me roses and Reese's Pieces." You can imagine the shock she felt when she opened the door and there, standing before her, is her boyfriend holding- you got it - ROSES AND REESE'S PIECES!

When she shared this story with me, I told her that Jesus is really laughing right now. He got her on that one!

Welcome to the world of friendship on a down-to-earth level with Jesus——the King of Kings, Ruler of Nations, Master of the Universe - yet still keeper of my heart, joy of my life and the dancing partner of my soul. He is IN our lives- not above, nor around, or at a distance. As my dear friend would say, "He Loves to be included!" Amen and Amen!

The famous
'Reese's Pieces and Roses

Our youngest daughter,
the lovely Faith. . .our prayed
for miracle baby girl!

THE CHINA CABINET
(January 20, 2015)

———◦ℴℴℴ———

C hange is sometimes painful- yet sometimes good. Because of a computer desk and chair that now reside in our great room- it became excruciatingly apparent that something had to be removed from the room. After touring several rooms in the house, hoping to find a bare corner for my china cabinet- THE CHINA CABINET- the one my precious mom had given to me many years ago, I resolved myself to selling it. Then after barely getting into the ordeal of measuring and posting on Craig's List- I became a tearful mess and soon the whole idea became abandoned, until now. For some reason, I felt ready to give it another try. I emptied the shelves and drawers, and found new places for all the years of collection that had so proudly been displayed. I relived some 30 plus years ago when my precious mom had announced, "Dee, you know what you need is a china cabinet. Here is some money, now go buy yourself one." I did just that- purchased a lovely corner china cabinet- unfinished-and stained it a beautiful oak color. It traveled with us on several moves after that- still maintaining that beautiful homey look. Now I was ready to post it for sale. Within just a few minutes, I was getting some interest. I looked at my lovely sentimentally cherished treasure and asked Jesus to choose someone special to buy it. That next evening I was to learn just how much He really does hear our prayers—all of them—no matter how big, no matter how small. At approximately 3:45PM the man arrived to pick it up. I knew immediately He was a Christian. He was to bring it home for his wife. As I helped him move it to his min-van, I shared with him the china cabinet story and asked him to share it with his wife. He then told me that they too were Christians and loved the Lord as well. I told him I had prayed that Jesus would pick the right family to buy my cabinet treasure. We both were blessed that He cares so much for His people. A couple hours later, I received a wonderfully encouraging e-mail from his wife- thanking me for the story and revealing that she feels a special 'attachment' to the china cabinet.

My faith has been jolted into high gear. Lord Jesus you are so into our lives- that is if we let You in.

Thank you for reminding me how much you love being included.

My Dearest Precious Rachie Bachie- January 31st, 2015
(in celebration of my granddaughter turning 13!)

Happy Birthday to you sweetheart- oh I so wish I could be there with you, hug you, and see your gorgeous smiling face. But I am honored to be asked to share a bit of myself with you via this smart phone. I am supposed to pass on to you my recollections in transitioning from girlhood to womanhood when I was turning 13 years old. (Can you even believe Grandma was once 13 years old?) So I have been gathering my thoughts throughout the day- trying to put my heart-thoughts into words—it is not the easiest. But here is my humble attempt.

I was in the 7th grade at Swanson Elementary School (no I did not attend a Junior High). I had met a best friend named Tonya White. We did everything together. I was painfully shy around boys and could barely look at them in the face. I felt okay about myself and enjoyed ice skating, biking, playing with my dogs, Barbie dolls (yes, your grandma loved dolls even at that age- I must admit) and shopping for clothes. (even then your grandma was becoming a clothes-aholic). I did some babysitting, had sleep-overs, parties, and spent a bit too much time talking to my friends during class instead of studying. It was also the year of the worst teacher I had ever had. He played favorites and I assure you I was not one of them. He made me feel small, stupid and unloved. But Jesus had already made His way to my heart so I had a best friend connection with Him even then.

As I look back on those years, I see myself as a little girl but not really little, a young woman, but still in some ways wanting to remain that little girl- To me, Rachel, it was a time of taking one step forward, then reluctantly looking back - yet excitedly looking ahead—ever mixed emotions, sometimes liking myself, other times wishing I looked like someone else. Maybe if I smiled like her or if I had blond hair or long hair, or clothes like her's, or maybe if I were smarter, or prettier, or this or that - just not feeling comfortable in my own skin sometimes. There are some things that I know now that I really wish someone would have taken time to tell me then. Those things, my dear sweet one, I now want to tell you. Please treasure them, for they are, what I believe to be, nuggets of gold.

"Rachel, did you know that after God had designed and created you, He stood back and said, " Ah, this is a good and lovely miracle I have made, There will never ever be another lovely girl like this. I want her to shine with her light and glow with all the specifically chosen colors I have given to her. I hope she uses all the gifts I have given her, for there will never be the same combination of gifts like her's." Rachel, there will be people that will try to squash you and throw water on your colors. Please do not allow them to blow out your flame. And remember, your colors are water-proof and oh by the way, the more you wear your colors proudly, the more vibrant Jesus will make your colors to be. Walk in grace, love even when it hurts, forgive 70 X 7, try your hardest to include Him and see His fingerprints in each and every day; and finally, trust in the Lord with all your heart and soul. Seek Him above all else and know He has a personal plan for your life—He is faithful to guide you to just the right life-path specifically chosen for you.

Well, my sweet granddaughter, I love you and want you to know that I, your grandma, will always have a special place in my heart for you.

Happy Birthday Sweetheart
Grandma

ALYSSA

(January 31st, 2015)

———◈———

I met her the first day of school in my little pre-school classroom. I was drawn to her, infatuated by her familiar charm—familiar because she looked and acted so much like my precious granddaughter that I miss terribly dearly- Rachel (who is now 13 years old).

Alyssa brings me back to a time in my life when my little Rachel was that age and things were sweet, innocent and precious - so very precious.

As the weeks drift by, I find myself totally captivated by her ways, her charming expressions, her mature yet child-like comments. She has most assuredly stolen my heart.

Alyssa is brilliant yet very huggy-feely- 'buried in my lap' kind of child. She tries her hardest to hide her little self in and around me and it makes me laugh and feel loved. Could it be that we both are giving and receiving what we both are in need of?

There are no two ways about it—Alyssa colors my pre-school days with a charm and freshness all her own.

One day I was feeling sad. I began thinking about Alyssa and that in a blink of an eye she will know far more than I. She will travel and be schooled and become a successful business woman, or maybe even a doctor. For life is like that. Then Jesus spoke to me with words of hope and the promise of His Plan. He said, "Dee, what you are giving to Alyssa she will keep forever. She will never lose what you are pouring into her."

I started crying and even as I write this I begin crying all over again. It was just what I needed to stir me forward. So the other day I heard her say, "Mrs. Brown, I think you'd better pray for me." I asked her what was wrong and she answered that she didn't feel very good. I quickly placed her on my lap. As she rested her head on my shoulder, I whispered to her, "Alyssa, did you know that you can pray to Jesus any time you want to?" She innocently replied, "No, I didn't know that." So we both prayed and asked the Jesus who planned for us to spend this year together to please make Alyssa feel better.

Some say I am not "preparing" Alyssa for what is coming next year: the big K—KINDERGARTEN! But there's something inside of me that beckons me to give to her what her little spirit is so starving for- lap time, love time—presence, presence, presence. And so, for this year, I try to be the professional teacher that I know I need to be, yet I fight the compromise/ balance/

boundary dance for something more powerful than anything in this world—love. After all, can you think of a better way to be remembered by a child?

FAMILY QUOTES

"It's not the knowledge that you impart, but the love to her heart that she will always have and never lose."

Greg Brown

"Anyone can *give* love, but not everyone can make someone *feel* loved."

Christopher Brown

RUNNING OUT OF GRACE

(February 1, 2015)

———⟫⟫———

D id you ever have a season or a month or even a day when you felt your 'grace container' that usually sits full and plump nestled and tucked down deeply in your heart- has spilled over and emptied out? You sit looking at people that you know whom you've always made exceptions for, now you find yourself looking at in distain, judgment and animosity. But it does not end there. No! Your mind takes you on a trip to past hurts of past people of past episodes. After you have traveled that road for a bit, now it's time for your mouth to empty out all the garbage that had been collecting since this "season" began. You hear yourself spewing what you thought you would never ever say, and then you realize something is missing. At first it almost felt good to fire away—after all, you tell yourself, I've been holding on to this stuff waiting for just the right time to use this ammunition. But that "feel good" feeling now becomes "pseudo good" and the heart begins to become homesick for its lifeblood. It needs its lifeblood. Because of Grace, our Lord looks at us in robes of righteousness. Because of Grace, we can enter the throne room. And if He, our Father God, forgives us and remembers our sins no more, then it's that same grace that should carry us to return that grace to others.

I am on the landing strip of that graceless season now. True, there's still a bit of grimace, grit and scorn; and although I may leave that graceless place kicking and shoving, it will eventually wean its way out. That 'last drop' is right around the corner; and I will return to God's plan for me. Until then I have every certainty that He loves me through it—never judging, never pushing, always waiting.

As I take His hand He whispers, "Welcome back, Dee." So our journey continues.

ON THE LOOKING FORWARD TO

(Feb. 3, 2015)

—✺—

What is it about this? I remember wondering what is more electrifying, the looking forward to or the actual doing of whatever it is. I don't wonder any more. For I know it is the looking forward to. Here's how it goes. You begin the planning stage ie. where, when, and with whom? Once that is completed, you make the reservations. There, that's done. Ah, but the real fun is still to come. For as the weeks draw nearer, the excitement in the heart begins to expand. You are at work and you find yourself fantasizing—leaving for the trip, arriving, and all the various fun things in your mind's planning log. Sometimes even in the wee hours of the morning you begin thinking about it, and the twinges of excitement are ignited. But the highest peak comes the night before. I love my 'night before the trip' journal. I have had it for decades now. It's so fun to look back and read all the fun moments I have experienced just in the imagery I have conjured up that night before. And as I read about past pre-trips, I can once again experience the thrill of expectation.

I guess I will always be the 'looking forward to' kind of girl. If you look back at some of the major enjoyable moments in your life, you may also agree that the anticipation part of that particular memory ranks quite high.

But here's the key- that the fantasized mind video you've been playing in your head all the weeks prior to the trip, finally does play out to be just as fun as you'd imagined it to be.

I have found this to be almost a 50/50 success. I have imagined sitting at various restaurants at the best table in the house (round- tucked in the corner by a fireplace) only to be led to a rotten too small table either by the kitchen or some unattractive section of the restaurant- void of any ambiance or warmth. I have imagined long, 'peace-filled- tender- moments- of- interesting- conversations' type road trips that have instead come with arguing and tension. I think the next time I begin the planned event, I am going to place it in Jesus hands and ask Him to bless the trip, and protect my plans and imaginings.

So, though I realize true joy is in the living out of each day, for there are so many miracles in any given day- still I am grateful for those fun, inexpressibly joyful hiccups in life, known to Dee as 'The Looking Forward To's.'

A DAY I WILL ALWAYS REMEMBER
Saturday, February 7, 2015

———⟳———

I have a bucket list. I know I am not alone. It's interesting to listen to other people's dreams as well. I was able to complete my first one just recently- cross country skiing. But I did not know that Jesus had already set the gears in motion—that He was going to give me HIS PERFECT WINTER'S DAY! We (my sister, Dawn, my niece, Leah, and daughter Faith and I) drove to Whitnal Park in Franklin, Wisconsin in the early afternoon. The day danced with sunshine, warmth (temp. was around 42 degrees) and the most peaceful park I had ever seen. After having donned ourselves in boots, skis and poles, we headed out onto the trails. I knew in a moment's time that God had ordered my steps that day. I don't remember a more perfect winter's day. I so loved the sun- and how it warmed my body and also my spirit. We laughed, fell, persevered, took tons of pictures, and ended with hot chocolate to boot! I remember the freeing feeling to actually being able to experience something I had only talked about for decades. But what really brought this event to a new level in life-long experiences is that it was so obviously drenched in His handiwork. I have said many times that the key to feeling close to God is when one sees His fingerprints in each new day. Well, I would say this ski day was more like His 'Palm Prints'! So extravagantly gracious was His love that day—and I could not help but look up to Him in the sky (I do that a lot- I don't think people know what I'm doing when I do it) and smile. I have a special way of communicating to Him sometimes- All I know is that He gave me that day—and I will forever thank Him.

My Bucket List Dream is fulfilled-
Here I am with (from left to right)
daughter Faith, niece Leah,
and sister Dawn.
Feb. 2015

FAITH

(February 11, 2015)

—⁓—

I have a daughter that carries with her pieces of Heaven. She exudes a peace that no one else I know can. Her presence is light and her words are wise. She does not play around with pretenses and manipulative mind games. She is herself- nothing More; yet what she is pours out to overflowing- touching and drenching lives with her realness.

Sometimes she is not sure of herself- and needs to be reminded of her intense uniqueness- which stands out in a world of too many want-to-be's, fake-phonies, copy cats and mundane humdrum grays- but those who have the eyes to see and the spirit to feel her heavenly qualities, also have the witness to know she brings to this world *His* ways, just wrapped a bit differently- that's all.

I have watched her grow in grace, be stretched and almost consumed in life's struggles, and be nearly crushed under unbearable emotional pain. Still, she has risen above it all- soaring to yet new heights of victories, triumphs, and overcoming many a battles.

Faith has taken my hand, and we have peeked behind God's curtain. I have learned of spiritual truths and mysteries that far outreach most people's entire earthy journeys. Exploring new heights of God's mysteries with Faith is but just one of many show-stopping, eye-popping, mouth-opening wonders.

I guess, if I were to round off or sum up my Faith, I would say simply: She is a gorgeous young woman whom God is using to peel back the heavy worldly curtain of pride, prejudice, deceit and envy- and call it for what it is. Faith, she is my daughter and my friend. She means everything to me. I love you Faith. I prayed long and hard for you, with tears of faith and hope; and I thank my Jesus for you each day that I have breath.

"So I say to you, ask, and it will be given to you, seek, and you will find; knock, and it will be opened to you." (Luke 11:9 NKJV).

WHAT DOES JESUS SAY ABOUT IT?
(February 15, 2015)

—⟨∾⟩—

I always enjoy asking people this question. Many times they hesitate for a moment, then answer me with a somewhat obscure answer and I politely move on.

But to me, that is EVERTHING.

I have a special two-way communication with Jesus. It has not always been this way. Even as a child, I have loved to talk and write to Him; and I am very grateful for that. But over the past 7 or 8 years, God has encouraged me to go deeper, and with that has come a trusting ear that He is indeed trying to speak to me. There have been times when I questioned if what I was hearing were truly His words. I have a feeling I am not alone in this area. I remember one time a dear friend of mine was nearing her time to be with Him. She had been suffering and I had asked Him why He had not taken her home yet. I immediately heard Him say, "I have her." I recall feeling confused, because no one had called to inform me of this. We even made plans to visit her in the hospitial that evening—only to learn that she had been welcomed home in glory that same day. And when more and more life stories proved to be confirmations of what He was trying to tell me, I began walking deeper into the waters. It has been lovely. And I have seen a pattern or 'common denominator' in His style. He is gentle with me. He encourages me to return to the now of my life and not waist time in the mucky squalor of future worrying. He is light-hearted and often reminds me to do this or that. Like today, He lovingly told me to stay a little longer for that hug from my precious husband. So instead of rushing off after a quick embrace, I lingered and was ever so grateful for His guidance. That's just one example. He also is a shopper. Some times I bring Him with me to the store. I ask Him to help me find just the right gift for a chosen person. He brings me smack dab to the item (and always affordable). He comforts me, totally understands me, validates me, corrects me (ever so tenderly), and gives me insight into circumstances. I have heard Him laugh on several occasions. He also helps me view certain situations from His angle instead of my usual flat view point.

I remember my mother-in-law telling me, "He loves to be included." There is so much truth in that. It's really the beginning of inviting Him into our world (which is really His).

I invite you to join me in this exciting journey. The first few times you discuss something with Him, you may hear a 'thought' and think it is just you. But that is where the trust comes in. Picture falling into someone's arms (trusting they will catch you). That's how this is. There has got to come a time when you venture out and 'go with' what your heart is hearing. And I promise you, the more often you trust, the easier it becomes. He absolutely loves to talk to you—He has volumes He's been waiting to tell you. We do not serve a silent, 'man of few words' type of God. Oh and one more thing, remember, He never slumbers. So, when those night terrors or anxiety attacks hit, just to whisper His name brings His presence; and sweet words of comfort come spilling out to blanket you with His tender peace. I hope that the next time someone asks YOU, "What does Jesus say about it?" You will answer emphatically, "He has much to say, and I am listening."

'AT THIS STAGE IN THE GAME'
(February 22, 2015)

—◦◦◦—

I was talking with my oldest daughter yesterday. We were on the subject of 'cheap airline tickets.' I'd mentioned a particular airline that I would not stoop to take even though their fares are major cheapo. I'd added, 'Girl, at this stage in the game, I'm just not going to stoop to the inconveniences of that airline.'

She laughed and reminded me of the multi million times I had used that expression while she was growing up. She'd recalled a time when I was using Estee Lauder cosmetics. She'd asked why I didn't use Maybelline? (to save money). She recalled my reply to be exactly the same, 'Girl, at this stage in the game . .'

We both laughed, because when I'd said that, I was only the age that she is presently!

So it got me to thinking: 'At this stage in the game.' What am I really trying to say - what am I trying to convey with those words? And I know. I have reasoned things out, and concluded that in my lifetime, I had scrimped, 'Greyhound' & 'Mega bused,' Motel 6, Atlantic Mills, and Fantastic Sams. And I had determined I owed it to myself and have now earned various extravagances. I am thinking I am not the only one with this mentality. But what exactly constitutes 'earned'?

Truthfully, it sounds haughty and smug. We really don't 'earn' anything—because everything is a blessing from our Lord. Somewhere in my mind, I feel if I sacrifice enough, I can go for the 'cherry on the top.'

Deep inside, I know it's all ridiculous. And thanks be to Jesus for His grace. I probably will continue to use that expression, continue to bait and switch, still enjoy a nice hotel room, JJill clothes and Spalon Montage hair cuts, Ugg and Coach, and various foods at Byerly's. But I am not altogether hopeless, There does also remain that element of saving big as well. Anyone want to join me for a stop at the Good Will? After all, it's right down the road?

ONE LEG AT A TIME

February 24, 2015

—◦◦◦—

T he first time I heard this expression was when I was talking with my daughter about a haughty know-it-all doctor she had been working with. She had felt belittled through an unfortunate situation with this person. But her statement told me she had managed to rise about the circumstance and see it in a big picture. "After all, mom," she had concluded, "He puts his pants on one leg at a time, just like everybody else." Wow- that clearly brought him down from his high horse to a mere step stool, I would say. And it is a most healthy way to view all people whom we are tempted to worship, take glory in and lift up high. Mostly, it helps me put everyone in the proper perspective. I have a weak link in this area. I can easily fall prey to various Hollywood stars, famous musicians and anyone whom I highly admire. It is not hard for me to have them flying high right up to the top of the ladder, as I sit there, mouth open, oooing and awing them in a most unhealthy way. Then I think, 'wait a minute,' they are people, to be enjoyed, appreciated and admired. But they are NOT to be worshipped.

Ego is an interesting thing. People are always talking about their 'ego.' Webster describes it as: 'the conscious self.' Then right beneath that word comes: 'egocentric: self-centered, caring only for one's own interests.' Seems to me it can be a slippery slope to be at a healthy ego only to discover one has (sub)consciously slid down into 'egocentric.' I recall Jesus saying, "If anyone desires to come after Me, let him deny himself, and take up his cross, and follow me. For whoever desires to save his life will lose it, but whoever loses his life for my sake will find it. For what profit is it to a man if he gains the whole world and loses his soul? (Matt. 16:25–26 NKJV)

"Yes, all of you be submissive and be clothed with humility, for God resists the proud but gives grace to the humble. Therefore humble yourselves under the mighty hand of God- that He may exalt you in due time, casting all you cares upon Him, for He cares for you." (1 Peter 5:6 NKJV).

My prayer is that the Lord will allow me enough grace and favor to keep me grateful and joyful, but enough challenges to keep me on my knees, looking up, and humble.

Yep, that pretty much sums it up for all of us who feel like we're climbing the ladder to stardom. 'One leg at a time, all of us, one leg at a time!'

CHILDREN ARE POETS
(March 8, 2015)

—⟨♫♫⟩—

It seems I have known that children are born poets for several years now. I recall the day a little 4 year old came running to me (a pre-school teacher), reporting that one of his classmates had 'leaky eyes.' I never forgot that. It sounded so precious-yet I got the point. Yes indeed that little girl was crying.

I believe children teach us not only how to express ourselves in a poetic manner. They also teach the world in countless ways how to live, love and stay real- in amongst a world that presses in on them from every side with facades, counterfeit emotions, and plastic lifestyles. I watch them, listen to them and enjoy their realism.

Seeing the world through a child's eyes can be purifying, exhilarating and freeing. Their presence can fill a room with a host of angels- whose job is to guard them and praise our Lord in the Throne room.

We now have a new baby in our family. My son and daughter in law have welcomed in a brand new baby boy. His big brother, (3 ½ years old), is currently in the transition stage of adjusting to this new little micro- member. He is learning about this new little life that shares his room, his mommy and daddy, his dining room table, his time, and his car. And he is here to stay. When they left him with family to be cared for while the mommy and daddy were in the hospital with the birth of the new one, he found it extremely emotionally painful to let daddy go to be with mommy. Daddy tried his best to comfort him. He told him to be brave and strong. He loved on him, hugged him and tucked him into his little bed. But as hard as he tried, comfort would not come. Finally, quite apologetically, our little man looked up at his daddy and replied, "Daddy, I can't stop the sad from coming out of my eyes."

And to this I say, "My sweet little one, we adults know how You feel, just never quite knew how to express it until now!"

"Take heed that you do not despise one of these little ones, for I say to you that in heaven their angels always see the face of My Father who is in heaven" (Matt. 18:10 NKJV)

THE FLIP SIDE
(March 31st, 2015)

—⁓—

I remember as a young girl buying my first 45 LPN record. I could not wait to get home and play it on my record player/ stereo. Oh how I'd be swept away by its crooning. I would listen to it as loudly and as often as I pleased. But I also discovered something that came with my special treasure, the 'other song' on the 'other side' (also commonly known as the 'flip side') The songs were always (and I do mean always) horrible. They were non heard-of's and boring- an extreme contrast to what I had personally chosen. But I would pacify myself with the fact that the bad comes with the good.

It's been over 50 years since those record-playing years. But there is indeed an analogy that can be sifted out of the past. Doesn't everything in life seem to have a 'flip side' to it? Allow me to explain.

Take for example an upcoming, long- awaited vacation. You plan for it, visualize snippets of it, pack and breathe in every anticipated moment. The time flies and you try your hardest to recreate it in your mind as you make the journey home. Here comes the flip side: unpacking, facing the realities in life, and watching as the golden carriage gets replaced with pumpkins and mice. Sometimes it seems life is like this. The song we hear is not the one we chose to listen to. But because of Jesus, He gives us a new song - a song specifically chosen for us. Faith reminds me that life won't always be on the flip side. So as I return the suitcases back to their rightful place in the basement, I think to myself, ' You know those LPN's that I would purchase even though the flip side songs were catastrophic in taste, were all worth it. After all, hearing the favorites on the chosen side made it all worthwhile—I can tolerate the flip, because I know what is on the other side!

THIS THING CALLED GRACE
April 9, 2015

—⁓—

I love this word. It is a beautiful name. It is the name given to my lovely granddaughter by Jesus Himself, while she was still within the womb. I also love speaking this word - even wearing this word. However, 'doing' this word puts an entirely different slant on it. Hmmmm, I am so for asking people to 'give me' grace. Sometimes, I almost expect them to - like I've earned it or something. But then I remember- the very thought that grace can be earned in actuality erases the word. Because grace is grace. It can never ever be earned. It is a gift given without money, no strings attached, free and clear; and we with our human earthly brains cannot fathom this very easily. After all, isn't everything at one point or another earned? We earn love, paychecks, smiles and hugs, respect, trust, etc. etc. So this thing known as grace, I don't really know what to do with it, what shelf to store it on, or what subject to place it under. It is like it's this word that's right before me - yet so very far away. Why? Why is this so far-reaching? Is it because I struggle with its command? The very word, spoken ever so softly carries with it a strong and mighty decree to all who take it seriously, to all who swallow its intent, to all who thoroughly digest it.

Jesus showed us how in the most poignantly graphic way He could. Can I not do my part to follow His example. I try so hard - yet it seems so little.

And so I discover that by giving it away, I am far richer than I could ever imagine. I feel lighter and perhaps the more I give This grace away, the easier it will be the next time. Grace, if you think about it, isn't it synonymous with the name Jesus? Grace- I am so nothing without it.

Lord, fill us with Your Grace so that we forever have more than enough to give away.

"My Grace is sufficient for you, for My strength is made perfect in weakness." (2 Cor. 12:9 NKJV)

A WHEELCHAIR KIND OF LOVE
(May 3, 2015)

—⟨ν⟩—

I t was a hard visit. Funeral arrangements had to be made. Things were being disclosed and hidden secrets that were once turned inside out now were being exposed. Each day came with its own burdens and overwhelming disappointments. What was once believed to be so, now reared its ugly head and seemed to scream, "I fooled you, you thought that, but it's really this." The pain was deep and cutting. But the most painful question remained, 'Did his father love him?'

I remember when he said it. "Dee, I guess my father never really loved me at all." I had so wanted to disagree, to disprove this harsh statement. But I couldn't. I wondered myself.

Then I came upon a flyer I'd received about a race my daughter and I would be running in—(Race for the Cure). It mentioned: The Wheelchair Race. I began thinking about that. I reasoned that even though those disabled people would be 'running this race' a bit differently, still they would be 'racing' for the same goal, purpose, and reason as the rest of us.

I thought about how each individual loves differently and in different degrees. Some people show visibly extravagant body language when it comes to loving. Still others are subtle, quietly displaying their love in gentle ways. But some, because of various pasts, can only give love via a broken and disjointed style. They cannot give what they do not have, so they give 'wheelchair style.'

When I mentioned this to him, he looked at me and I saw a hint of hope and healing in his eyes.

Perhaps it would help if we looked at all people this way. Some people are marathon runners, swooping down love on everyone they meet. Some people are walkers, cautiously reaching out with a bit of hesitancy in their gait. But some people have never even learned to walk at all. They are the people that need to be taught, carried part way, then held, encouraged and believed in.

His dad could only give what he had. And although it was not what most people would call unconditional love, it was love- bruised, faltering, and skinned knee in appearance, but it still was love.

Who are we to judge the extent of love one has for another. The best we can do is gladly receive whatever is given.

So the next time someone you know does not quite make the high bar you have set for him, remember, perhaps all he can give is a WHEELCHAIR KIND OF LOVE!

IN CELEBRATION OF GRANDMA'S PRECIOUS NATALIE WENDEE

June 6, 2015

—⟨∞⟩—

Congratulations Natals on turning 12 years old. You have arrived at a beautifully and crucially important place; for it is around this time that you begin to question some things, yet find answers to others. Some of your hopes and dreams may take on a new reality; yet new ones come to birth as well. There may be deep tears, but there will also come joys yet to be experienced. You are entering a most memorable season of your life.

When the Lord Jesus planned for your arrival here on the earth planet, He knew the world needed more kindness, thoughtfulness, a spirit of tenderness, compassion and sacrificial love. He created YOU to teach the world such things as these. And you have taught well. You are lovely. Your beauty far exceeds most young girls. But to me, far more gorgeous than any outward appearance, is your heart. For it is there that the richest of beauty outshines any and all other imposters. When I look at you, I see so much more than your sweet smile and warm eyes. I see inside to a little girl in midstream of becoming a woman. I wonder and imagine what you will be like when you have reached womanhood. And sometimes I think I already know. But whatever path the Lord may someday lead you on, I pray you hold tightly to His hand. Never allow the world to loosen your grip, and walk and talk with Him along the way. I promise you the journey of a lifetime.

Thank you Natals, for giving me the ultimate privilege of being your grandma. And I look forward to the amazing blessing of watching the beautiful flower that you are— blossom into all the fragrant splendor that only Jesus could make you to be.

When I was lying in bed, thinking of what to write to you, this is the Bible verse that came to mind for you. I believe it is from Jesus:

"Finally, brethren, whatever things are true, whatever things are noble, whatever things are just, whatever things are pure, whatever things are lovely, whatever things are of good report, if there is any virtue and if there is anything praiseworthy, meditate on these things." (Phil. 4:8 NKJV)

I love you dearly Natals,
Grandma

THE TREASURE HUNT
May 29, 2015

—◈—

I so enjoy looking at life in metaphoric ways. It not only softens the inevitably hard, inconsistent and unexplainable happenings in life; but it also helps me make sense of it all. This one is my favorite:

I like to think of each day the Lord Jesus gives me as a new day with a fresh treasure map. And each one of those days comes with hidden treasures that He has personally and specifically placed for each one of us. Consider them little personal winks from Him. Do not laugh - but sometimes (well actually all of the time) when I discover one He'd hidden for me to find, I look up to heaven at Him. Perhaps you have even been with me when you've seen me do this. It's my way of letting Him know that 'I got that one'!

It's hard to predetermine just how, or when we find these hidden gems. Some days I find more than others. It's really not about navigational skills; what it IS about is staying tuned in to the Holy Spirit's presence and keeping one's eyes and ears open to the things of the spirit. There are subtleties that He places in our paths and it is our job to do the searching.

So come with me. We'll hold hands and walk this treasure hunt together. Though the treasures that you find may look different from mine, we will have one thing in common- they're all from the same PAPA!

SIGNATURE PEOPLE

(June, 2015)

—⟨⟨⟩⟩—

We all know 'signature people.' They are the ones that come to your mind when you hear a particular song or word, watch a certain movie, see a kind of jewelry, smell a particular fragrance, visit a certain place, read a certain book etc. etc. etc. I was just thinking today of all the 'signatures' I have treasured of various people in my life; For example, my precious mother. Each time I see turquoise I think of her. (It was her favorite kind of jewelry). The very word: 'antiques' brings to my mind my awesome sister (the lover of antiques). Or what about chic peas. This was one of my dad's favorite foods. I have a friend who loves polka dots and another one super into Pansy flowers. Then there's my daughter in law - and her love of the beach; her turquoise blue spreads softly throughout her home. Signatures can also be captured with actors and singing groups.

When I hear 'Bill Gaither,' I think of two people- my mother in law and our son. Both of them so love that group!

I know you too could fill in the blanks on all the 'signature people' in your life as well. It's something all of us never set out to deliberately be known for, but it happens and then we 'become the owners,' of it. (whatever that may be). Think about this - what are yours?

WALNUTS, TURKEY, YOGURT, AND DARK CHOCOLATE!

(June 1, 2015)

———✺———

You know sometimes we read people wrong. I think it's because we have pictured in our minds how someone should react to our needs; and when their actions don't quite fit into the mold we have fashioned for them, we come up short. It happened to me just today.

When the demonic and angry spirit of depression attacked me a short time ago, I had unwittingly devised an 'agenda' of how my husband should treat me (which includes a broad and massive spectrum of expectations). If those expectations are not met, then a conclusion is often drawn that can be as far from truth as Neptune is from Mercury! I had been pouting all day about it. Then he returns home from work holding a bag of stuff. He looks at me and declares, "I got some stuff for you." His eyes are sparkling and I am reminded of the many times he's brought home roses. I look at him solemnly. He proceeds to pull out the 'stuff.' First on the list is a turkey loaf, next a large bag of walnuts, followed by a hefty bag of dark chocolate, and last but certainly not least, a 24 oz. carton of Greek Yogurt. He looks at me and declares, "Did you get my e-mail? I went on line and found out foods that help depression." In that instant I felt my heart go from rocks of ice to a warm pool of love, appreciation and awe. Whoa Dee, what part of caring for you do you not see here?

So then it is probably safe to say that each person has their own set of crayons on how they choose to color those they love that are hurting. And though we want to pick up a particular color, hand it to the person and emphatically tell them to 'use this color on me.' We cannot. But what we can do is appreciate any color used; for each person cares in different ways. I am learning to keep my hands off of other people's color crayons, and look at people and situations with new eyes.

THERE'S SOMETHING ABOUT THE EYES
(June 25, 2015)

———✻———

I t's true. There IS something about people's eyes. With each grandchild, I have found the hereditary 'link' in the eyes. It's the first thing I look for when they're born. I see past generations in their eyes.

I am the type of person that looks into people's eyes when I speak to them. It tells me much about them. In the Bible it says that the window to the soul is through one's eyes. I recall people saying,(when in doubt about the authenticity of the words of the other person), 'look at me and tell me that.' This tells me that to be able to deceive someone verbally when you are looking at them is more difficult than if one is speaking via the phone, e-mail or text.

Another aspect of the eyes is it is also the tell-tale part of the body that ages first. It speaks also of little sleep, worry, depression and anxiety. It has a silent voice–yet loud to the observer. Why do so many people wear sunglasses on cloudy days and inside buildings? For all the many reasons people may give, it is my hunch that the wearing of sunglasses hides their story. Sunglasses have attitude - and the world sometimes appears to be abundant in that category.

The next time you are given the blessing of listening to someone pour out their heart, listen to their eyes. They may reveal to you more than their words ever could.

THERE REALLY IS
POWER IN PRAISE
(Sept. 2014)

———❧❧❧———

On Sunday, October 5th the 3 of us (Greg, our daughter Faith, and I) experienced a most traumatic event. The following is our story.

The afternoon of September 23rd proved very exciting—as we boarded the plane that would take us on our long awaited dream trip to Europe. While there, the days flew by as we felt God continually rolling out the red carpet for us in so many ways. But upon arriving at the train depot in Milan, Italy, things drastically shifted. At approximately 8:00 PM on Oct 5th, we found ourselves victims of theft by 4 gypsies who tripped Greg, stealing his wallet and all of our cash for our trip. I remember standing there, feeling ever so violated and vulnerable to the passers by and saying, 'Jesus, help us.' As we sat in the police station, I felt the Lord saying to me, "Thank me in this." I then recalled the song by Casting Crowns 'Praise You in the Storm' and decided to do just that; and that is when the supernatural moving of the Holy Spirit kicked in—for as I praised Him, my voice was continually busy with numerous things to thank Him for - on and on I went. By the time I was done, I felt different, like we were on the winning side.

Time does not allow me to tell you all the events that followed that were like healing balm of blessings. That evening Jesus said, "Now Dee, I want you to go on a treasure hunt for the remaining part of your trip. I have many surprise blessings still waiting for you to discover." And that is just what happened. Gifts upon gifts were placed before us in countless ways.

"I will lift up my eyes to the hills from whence comes my help? My help comes from the Lord, Who made heaven and earth." (Ps. 121:1–2 NKJV)

Husband Greg and daughter
Faith with me- posing in front
of the Coliseum in Rome.
September/ October 2014

I HAVE KNOWN YOU

Happy Birthday to the love of my life!

(March 31, 2015)

I have known you as a boy—with brown bangs that flirtatiously brushed your forehead - a boy that played an electric guitar-songs I'd love to hear once more- dreams big, gives big and and loves big. I have known you as a man - a man with great talents I'd not known before, an awesome gift of writing, of inventing, of being one of the finest engineers there ever was and ever will be. I have known you as a Godly husband, who walked the plank but did not drown - who believes that prayer does indeed move mountains and has seen it to be so. I have known you as a man of courage, of strength and optimism.

I have loved you through the years of boyhood into man-hood-and I will always love you, always need you, always feel my happiest when I am near you—

I thank my Lord for you and pray you always know how wide and high and deep this woman that writes this feels about you.

I have known you. I have loved you- and I cherish you more than I can express.

Happy Birthday Minser!

With love from your Bunners.

ON THE GRADUATION OF MY SISTER FORM ALVERNO COLLEGE- WITH A BACHELOR OF SCIENCE DEGREE IN NURSING- AS AN RN

(May 19, 2012)

—◦◦◦—

My Dear Precious Priceless Sister: Cutie

I have visualized this moment more times than you will ever know. I would envision myself standing before a group of people, sharing from my heart what I had collected through out these 7 years—some things I have written down—others just remained embedded in my heart—waiting for the opportune time to be birthed. So please grant me a few minutes of sharing.

Dawn, I remember that 'phone call' -the one where you said, "Dee, I think God told me today that He wants me to go back to ~ ool and be a nurse." I heard some hesitation in your voice, perhaps waiting for my reaction, but I also heard a conviction, like you were about to set sail and wanted my blessing. I readily gave that to you, and remember saying, 'Dawn, if the Lord is in on this, then you shall succeed, because He's on your side, and no one can stop God's plan. No matter how hard they try.' And they did try, but you trudged through the sludge of harassment, were faced countless times with integrity choices, struggled with certain professors that probably should not be teaching, sleepless nights and way too early mornings—and through it all, you wore the hat of mother, sister, friend, and landlord. You never once compromised your convictions, and trusted the God who first called you to join Him in this journey.

I recall phone calls. We'd talk health issues. I could bet on it that at some point in the conversation you would say, with enthusiastic certainty and confidence, "Oh, I know all about that."

Remember the times when you would ask over and over and over again, "Do you really believe I will graduate, Dee? How can you be so sure all the time? You say it like you're so sure?" And I would reply, 'I keep having this vision of you, wearing a white coat with your name on the front and an RN after it—and you're walking into a patient's hospital room, and introducing yourself.'

Or what about all those situations when it was so totally obvious that Jesus had moved yet another mountain on your behalf. We both, mouths wide open, would be absolutely awed by His love for you.

Cutie, I want you to know that less than 2% of the human race ever live long enough to fulfill their life long dreams! You did it, Cutie, you did it!

So, sweet sister of mine, I want you to know how very proud I am of you. Now you are on the runway ready to burst forth with all the charisma and gusto the Lord has blessed you with— and my dear priceless sister, remember, I WILL BE CHEERING WHEN YOU FLY!

I love you Cutie, Sis

"The Lord is your keeper; The lord is your shade at your right hand. The sun shall not strike you by day. Nor the moon by night." (Ps. 121:5–6 NKJV)

THAT WAS FOR ME -
YOU DID THAT FOR ME
(January 12, 2015)

—◦◦◦—

I had arrived especially early that Monday morning, hoping to prepare my pre-school classroom for the week. But Jesus had other plans. I had no more than stepped into my room when I heard pain-filled crying coming from the nearby classroom. I quickly followed the sound and anxiously asked my friend, who was the early morning care-giver, 'What's wrong?' I learned that her sweet little grandson had not worn gloves in route to school and now he was in tremendous pain. Cold weather had put a gripping vice on us Minnesotans for the past week; and I knew the weather was in the single digits—with the wind chill below zero. I quickly snatched him up (didn't even take time to remove my coat) and placed him on my lap in my rocking chair. Then I wrapped his tender little red hands in my scarf. He immediately calmed down. We rocked and he whimpered and it wasn't long before he was ready to return to his grandma. As I returned to my room, even though precious 'early morning time' had drifted by, I couldn't help but predict what would happen. I had seen it before. When we do something for someone else we miraculously have what seems 'extra time' to get the stuff done we had initially planned to complete. And I was right. When it was finally time for my students to enter my classroom, I was completely ready. It is strange how that works. When we give ourselves (and our time) to someone else in place of our own pre-planned agenda, God gives us bonus minutes!

The next morning, as I drove to work, I heard Him say, "You know Dee, that was for Me. You did that for me. You warmed MY hands. You rocked ME. You comforted ME." And as my eyes welled with grateful tears, I was reminded once again that when we do things for others, we are truly doing them for Him.

"Then the King will say to those on His right hand, 'Come, you blessed of My Father, inherit the kingdom prepared for you from the foundation of the world; for I was hungry and you gave Me food; I was thirsty and you gave Me drink; I was a stranger and you took Me in; I was naked and you clothed Me; I was sick and you visited Me; I was in prison and you came to me.'" (Matt. 25:34–36 NKJV)

TIRED OF BEING AFRAID

—◆—

The day could not have been more perfect. We were vacationing with our family- the family who had moved to Redding, California.

We had decided to rent a pontoon and cool off a bit on the lake. Everyone had brought their swim suits (well, not everyone—not me). When the time seemed right, the family started jumping in, splashing around and laughing like crazy. I sat there, feeling like I had not been 'asked to the party.' Finally, my granddaughter asked, "Grandma, why don't you come in?" To which I replied, 'Because I'm afraid of deep water.' (although I can swim, deep water is SO not my comfort zone), plus my son in law had estimated the depth to be somewhere around 50–60 feet- (I did so not want to know that!) Then suddenly, out of nowhere, my daughter looked at me and said, "You want to go in, don't you?" How did she know? I answered her honestly, 'Yes.' I had not brought my suit, but whatever, there's no rule about jumping in with one's shorts and shirt on! Then there began a plan. Tami, my daughter, would jump in with me. When we were about to jump, grandson Ben interrupted with a need. Before Tami could turn around, I had jumped! (the horrendous feeling of waiting became too great). After I jumped in, Tami looked at me and asked, "Mom, I'm curious, what possessed, oops, wrong word - what inspired you to do this?" To which I replied, 'I'm tired of being afraid.'

"For God has not given us a spirit of fear, but of power and of love and of a sound mind." (2 Tim. 1:7 NKJV)

"For we walk by faith, not by sight." (2 Cor. 5:7 NKJV)

And Jesus' promise to all of us is: "And lo, I am with you always, even to the end of the age." Amen (Matt. 28:20 NKJV)

'Now to Him who is able to do exceedingly abundantly above all that we ask or think according to the power that works in us, to Him be glory in the church of Christ Jesus to all generations forever and ever. Amen." (Eph. 3:20 NKJV)

EVERYBODY'S WATCHING

—⟆⟆—

Am I the only one who seems 'stuck in the mud' on this area? I think I know its origin. I recall hearing my mom say to me on occasion, "I feel everyone is looking at me." Perhaps I adopted that feeling, without even giving my approval. I remember a dear pastor reassuring me, "Dee, believe me, everyone is into their own lives, they are not watching you." I really liked that. It was freeing. But the freedom stayed for only a short span.

Really, what is my problem? I mean, do I really think that the world is out there with their binoculars watching my every move?

I believe all weird quirks, such as this and others, are rooted from some traumatic event. I know for me it was from an extended time of teasing and intense bullying—but I also know it is time to break free and fly. Think of the things you've missed out on, just because you thought, "What would people think?"

I have actually done just that. I remember a time when after leaving a grocery story with my cart of food, I put my two feet on the back and went 'motoring' down the parking lot. Someone once told me that the people we feel so intimidated by we will probably never ever see again.

It is good to be free of fears and the fear of people can be suffocating indeed! But there is ONE PERSON who IS watching, cares, and is in constant surveillance of me (and I love it)—Jesus reminds us in Luke 12: 6–7 (NIV) "Are not five sparrows sold for two pennies? Yet not one of them is forgotten by God. Indeed, the very hairs of your head are all numbered. Don't be afraid, you are worth more than many sparrows."

THE PLAN/ BEYOND THE CURTAIN

—◦◦◦—

S ometimes in life, actually, a great deal of times in life, things just don't seem to make sense. We cry out to God, "Why? I don't understand, what is the point? What is the reason? Where are we going with this, what am I supposed to be learning and is there even anything to be learning through this? Is this wasted pain? I don't understand God!" But what we don't know nor do we see, is that somewhere beyond the curtain, there is a plan. There IS a plan. This morning at church God gave me a vision. I saw what appeared to be a solid gold bar covered with a wispy layer of sand and dirt. Then a wind came and blew the sand and dirt off the gold bar- to reveal the gold, in all of its bright sparkling splendor. I felt the Lord showing me that just as iron sharpens iron—so it is with this- that although I am trudging through the dirt, God is in the process of refining me. He knew that only by traveling through those rough places can we be as refined and purified gold. This process hurts; but if we know He has a plan, then we can also know He will see us through. The pain, the Plan, the refined gold and the promise. Let us continue on this journey.

"Weeping may endure for a night, but joy comes in the morning." (Ps. 30:5 NKJV)

"For I know the plans I have for you," declares the Lord, "plans to prosper you and not to harm you, plans to give you hope and a future. Then you will call upon Me and come and pray to Me, and I will listen to you. You will seek Me and find Me when you seek Me with all your heart " (Jer. 29:11–13 NIV)

THE SHIP
AN ALLEGORY

—◁◊▷—

You see there was this ship. It was small yet powerful. Its purpose was to transport food and necessary supplies to other boats in various places in the seas. It didn't matter the size, color, or age of the boats. This little boat saw only one mission—to get the needed provisions to the awaiting crafts. Oh this boat was good, efficient, rugged and strong. In fact, too good. For the boats receiving the goods began to believe that this 'mighty ship' WAS the supplier. After some time, this little ship began to feel larger than it really was. It took time shining itself up, complete with a new paint job and steering wheel! The ship loved the praise and even considered moving on to 'more important business careers.'

And then it happened. A storm arose. It was a storm of all storms. As the little ship pressed on, riding the torrential storm, trying its hardest to get to the other ships,—it realized it was too small to do this job alone. After radioing to the 'HEADQUARTERS' an SOS, help was quick at hand and the small ship was rescued.

The little ship knew what it had to do. It sped to all the rigs—with now two missions at hand. It continued to provide their goods—but it never stopped reminding them that 'he' was NOT their 'supply savior.' He was NOT the originator of their supplies, but was only the TRANSPORTER. He explained to them that even he needed the HEADQUARTER'S HELP and could not do this mission without its ever constant assistance. "We are all in this together," he would explain, " And I will eventually become shipwrecked and broken if I too do not remember one important truth; that Though I supply, I am not and never will be your Supplier"!
Matthew 20: 27–28 (NIV)

"And whoever wants to be first must be your slave- just as the Son of Man did not come to be served, but to serve and to give His life as a ransom for many."
Proverbs 16:18 (NIV)

"Pride goes before destruction, a haughty spirit before a fall."
Proverbs 11:2 (NIV)

"When pride comes, then comes disgrace, but with humility comes wisdom."

THE RACE TRACK AND THE COUNTRY GRAVEL ROAD

(August 27, 2015)

———

Her life was busy, and her days spent in fast motion. Her comings and her goings were flashes of light and I missed her presence. It's okay, I kept telling myself, I will be okay. But then why the tears? Then I heard His voice. "Dee, I made your heart. I designed it to be just this way. Don't hide your hurts. Don't be ashamed of your heart. It is by my design." I felt validated and loved. I saw the whole of it and realized the conflict. She was flying by at a speed I could barely decipher. And I was meandering down a country gravel road, kicking a few stones and gathering wild flowers. Maybe someday she will be able to slow down so we can be. Maybe someday time will look differently and she will join me as I travel my slow placed stride to nowhere in particular. Maybe. . .someday. . . . .

WEAR THE PEARLS

(July 26, 2015)

———⟨∾∾⟩———

I had this thing about preserving really nice things. . . like jewelry, clothes, towels, dishes, even furniture. I found a strange sort of joy in just knowing I owned them; never using them mind you, just owning them. I recall one day receiving a complement on a particular piece of clothing I was wearing. . .to which I replied, 'I have had this in my closet for a long time. . .it's the first time I am wearing it.'

And then I read a powerfully poignant writing by one of my favorite writers, that of the late Erma Bombeck.

Her words helped reshape my thinking. Life is ever so short. . . 'Dee, enjoy these gifts God has so generously placed on loan for you'.

This morning I took out those gorgeously elegant pearls that had been willed to me by my precious mother in law; and as I clasped them around my neck, I felt a peace. . .and a greater joy still to have broken free from the disease of preserving. Let us all live in the now of our lives; What we have been given is the promise of today. . . drink in the sweetness of today. . .never lose a drop. Tomorrow is promised to no one. . . .today. . . .for it is a priceless gift and oh so fleeting.

THIS IS IT. . . .LOOK!!!!

—⟨⟨⟩⟩—

Nine months of preparation for this moment. I had planned, envisioned, dreamed, felt life, prepared the room, sewn a quilt, attended natural childbirth classes, packed the suitcase, and climbed the rugged mountain known as 'labor'. But as I waited while nurses prepared me for delivery, I had forgotten one thing. . .one very important thing. The nurse on my left saved the day as she spoke, "Look, this is it, watch, look!"!!!!! I had completely forgotten to watch this magnificently miraculous moment in time. . . .I almost missed it. . .I almost missed it!

As I think back on that day, almost 41 years ago, I cannot help but liken it to life. There appears to be an intense parallel. Just recently I sat visiting with an 'engaged to be married' couple. The young woman shared how frustrating it is to wait; and that she wished the time would go faster. I could not help but share my heart with her.

Don't you think that we are so busy hurrying life along, we are missing the 'Nows' of life? It almost seems we are being fooled into thinking that this 'elusive destination' we are all so excited to arrive at will bring us to an imaginary Never Never Land. So what do we do? We begin planning another life marker. . .and once more push and shove life along. I see a daddy, wide strides, holding onto his little 4 year old. The child is running to keep up with daddy. What would happen if daddy looked down and slowed his pace, and instead matched his pace with the child's. I feel like we are all on this fast-moving jet airliner; The world is whizzing by and we can barely make out what anything is anymore. We are too busy getting to wherever. Could it be that we have become so intoxicated with speed, efficiency and destination that we are missing the flowers of life that have been so lovingly and strategically planted along the way.

To the couple whose weeks could not go faster for their wedding. . .to them I say: Revel in the 'Now' of your engagement. These moments are also golden, for you will never ever be in this time of your life again.

And to the world I say: Slow down, stop, listen, notice, look into people's eyes, laugh with someone, cry with someone, care, breathe, and know that life is too precious to spend your whole time 'flying' through. Take the risk, get off the race track, and just for a time try walking down a quiet country road. You will be amazed at the life you have been missing!

BIO

Wendee (Dee) Brown lives in Chanhassen, Minnesota with her husband and youngest daughter. She just completed her 29th year as a pre-school teacher and is loving every minute. Wendee and her husband have five children, thirteen grandchildren, and counting. They love traveling, and have traveled quite extensively throughout Australia, Europe, and Guatemala, but they are the first to declare their faithfulness to their Midwestern hometown. Wendee's love of writing goes back to her high school English classes, where the teacher enjoyed reading her work to the class. When she's not writing, she enjoys teaching, biking, shopping, dancing, boating, gardening, decorating, sewing, and traveling.

BIBLIOGRAPHY

1 Penn, William, "Some Fruits of Solitude" Kessinger Publishing, 2004

2 Browning, Elizabeth, "Aurora Leigh" Oxford University Press, 1998

3 Addison, Joseph, "Cato A Tragedy and Selected Essays" Liberty Fund Inc., 2004

INDEX

A: ON GRANDCHILDREN

B: PRE-SCHOOL STORIES

God Sightings

Teacher Sit by Me

The Conference

Mother's Tea

Love is Stronger Still

Behind the Transparent Curtain

Alyssa

That Was Me-You Did That For Me

C: OUR GOD'S BEAUTIFUL WORLD AND SEASONS

A Summer's Morning

Description of Autumn

The Last Rose of Summer

The World Wakes

Open Our Windows

Thoughts on Winter

Listen to a Chorus

God's Symphony

And So the Symphony Continues

Sequel to the Symphony

Summer's Entrance

Happy Birthday to my Boy

Lifesong

Happy Mother's Day

In Honor of Tami

The Departure

Happy Birthday Precious One of Mine

A Mother's Parable

The Big Sister

When God Changes the Weather

Nuts, Green Apples and Dish Soap

A Tribute to my Daughters

Happy Birthday Christoher Brownerella

A Prayer for my Christopher

Parents Are:

The Dedication of Cody

When God Answers Prayers

My Dear Precious Son

Roses and Reese's Pieces

A Day I Will Always Remember

Faith

On the Graduation of my Sister

My Dear Precious Daughter-My Tami Dawn

All the T's are Crossed-All the I's are Dotted

A Day at Walmart

A Tribute to all the People who Make Me Laugh

The Peacock Story

The Peacock Story Revisited

The Surprise Blessing

Are There Bicycles in Heaven?

Joshisms

The Time Man

I Love Saturday Mornings

Laughter is God's Medicine

The Serendipity

The Receptionist/The Party

Dr. Christmas Tree

The Color Gray

The Walking Zombies

An Angel Named Caroline

The High School Reunion

Gone to the Wind

Pop

Pennies in the Sawdust

Tough as Hide

When He Hides Surprises

When God Speaks

This Day

CPSIA information can be obtained
at www.ICGtesting.com
Printed in the USA
LVOW04s2142071115

461438LV00002B/3/P